Rise of the

WARRIOR LEADER

Ten Dimensions for Unshakeable Steward Leadership

CLAUDIO CHISTÈ

Published by TW Publishers

E-mail: hello@twpublishers.co.za *Website:* www.twpublishers.co.za
Office: +27647794326 / WhatsApp: +2764779432647
Thomas Street, Olifantsfontein, 1666 Midrand, South Africa

Cover design by Tendai Chidziya

Edited by John Dorrington

ISBN: 978-1-991219-79-4

e-ISBN: 978-0-6397-4971-6

www.centre-for-leadership.com

I

Claudio Chistè brings a new lens to the leadership domain, namely that of Steward-Warrior Leadership. This book provides a systems view of how a leader and leaders can significantly impact societal, organization and individual development outcomes through leading with purpose, wisdom and courage. His emphasis on leading during times of crisis and discontinuity is especially relevant for leading in the 21st century.

Shaun Rozyn
Managing Director, Executive Education & Lifelong Learning:
The Darden School Foundation
University of Virginia (USA)

This lively highly readable text is a stimulating contribution to skillful leadership and great guide for those either starting out on their role as leaders or those wanting to polish their skills. Claudio offers a special contribution in his addressing the 'both-and' perspective of strength and compassion, required by emotionally intelligent leaders managing in turbulent times. The emphasis on the importance of strong positive values and self-reflective awareness is a consistent theme in his setting out of the ten dimensions of Steward-Warrior Leadership. A unique contribution is Claudio's fascinating examples and stories of heroes and villains drawn from particularly South African history, illustrating the 'both-and' of exceptional relationally-intelligent leadership – courageous decision-making strength in crisis moments, and sociable engagement up and down the line in less stressful times. This is a timely contribution for coaches, students of coaching and leadership, as well as human resource practitioners and of course, every level of leader.

Dr Dorrian Aiken
Leadership Development Coach
Co-founder of Coaches & Mentors of South Africa (Comensa)
Lecturer M Phil in Leadership Coaching:
University of Stellenbosch Business School (USB)

The Steward-Warrior Leadership model provides a fresh perspective on leadership. In recent times, we have seen a resurgence in awareness of Servant Leadership and VUCA. However, this new model brings an Ownership-driven approach with actionable principles which can be easily implemented. The model focuses on personal and organisational culture to bring about group cohesion and a focus on the team. This enables adaptation and implementation, in order to adapt and effect change in these times of chaos and complexity. These principles are applicable across multiple sectors, be it corporate, sports, government, politics, military and our day to day lives.

Dr Roger Prentis
Partner of consultancy RDP International
Special Advisor, House of Lords (England, UK)

It has been my privilege to have a journey with the author. My knowledge of Claudio, coupled with our friendship, has only enriched my life. As our relationship grew, he engaged with his background knowledge and further study into leadership. His conceptual understanding of leadership is not only contextually valid but also applicable within current reality. The gems he has excavated in his research lead to the establishing of conceptual models that have a great relevance to leadership as a discipline. The author has furthermore drawn on data that will give the content good applicability in the leadership context. The leadership content provided is not only relevant but also very timely in the context of the worldwide leadership challenge. While there is no 'quick fix' with regard to our leadership challenge, I do believe that his work will have a significant benefit in the process. Congratulations with your work!

Dr Albert Wort
Qualification Leader - Personal Professional Leadership
Department of Industrial Psychology and People Management:
University of Johannesburg (South Africa)

This book makes a welcome contribution to present understanding of the multifaceted subject of leadership. It draws upon existing literature, including works by Drucker, Keohane and Nye, and Hershey and Blanchard, for historical context and to underpin its theoretical discussion. In this regard the book has firm foundations: it references past and present theories of leadership, with the aim of contributing practical and up-to-date perspectives.

Existing theoretical frameworks including Contingency Theory, stewardship theory, and Servant Leadership are explained and critiqued in a fresh and well-paced style. There is extensive use of tables, graphs, and images resulting in a visually engaging book. Quotes and summaries of philosophies provided from diverse sources such as Jack Welch, Austrian-American management consultant Peter Drucker, and Nobel Laureate Daniel Kahneman, give discussion of issues and questions a practical, lively, and relevant edge.

The Author has contextualised several of the topics within a uniquely African framework, nimbly moving the discussion from historical roots to the present day. From the Zulu leadership concept of *Isithunzi* to consideration of the unique personal skills and inspirational qualities of Nelson Mandela. The discussion of the four factors of Transformational Leadership delves into relevant models, including those by Patterson and Winston. The dangers presented by leaders who exhibited several of the traits discussed, but utilised them for evil purposes, including Hitler and Idi Amin, are highlighted and then developed further in the Chapter titled, the Dark Side of Leadership.

This book takes a fresh approach to the question of what makes for effective leadership; it challenges existing assumptions whilst at the same time building upon well-known models in the field. In this regard it is a useful, original, and insightful contribution to our understanding of the subject in all its forms.

Dr Simon Norton
Senior Lecturer, Cardiff Business School
Cardiff University (Wales, UK)

After reading *Rise of the Warrior Leader,* I am firmly under the impression that our current age is the most difficult era in world history in which to serve as a leader. Social media has pierced the vulnerable shield of leaders whereby anyone who can type with one finger is easily able to venture an opinion on a topic of which no experience or background knowledge is required. There is no necessity for a contributor to social media to provide evidence for an opinion, with no accountability required. It is challenging for our leaders and the unintended consequences are that fewer people are prepared to lift their heads above the parapet. Not only is this obvious in the workplace but is also particularly evident in volunteer organisations. This is the curse of our society today as the genuine leaders are reluctant to emerge and the vacuum is being filled with populist leaders spewing out inanities and tragically dividing our communities.

Claudio maintains that the situation all those years ago in caveman times revealed 'raw leadership'. Closeted in a cave and confined to small areas meant that there were no secrets, with weaknesses soon exposed. People depended on their leaders for safety and security. Good leaders earned their caveman stripes the hard way, although I suspect that anyone writing anti-leader slogans on a cave wall soon had short thrift. In that era, trust and faith in their leaders was built up around the cave campfire but that would go on to change in the period between Cave and Facebook as leaders hid over the intervening centuries behind high walls, uniformed troops and inherited privilege. Traditionally, it was about Centralised Command and Control. But that was before the ready access to information – through platforms such as social media - changed the leadership landscape....

In spite of a myriad of leadership books over the years, the question of leadership has traditionally been addressed as a transactional process following a linear sequence - a series of steps which an organisation should take to ensure success. The problem over the years has been the growing realisation that successful organisations are in fact dynamic - unpredictable, continually evolving and changing.

Tackling the problem by rigidly following a linear sequence of action was never going to cut the mustard. This book shows us that the Warrior Leader understands this, with convincing data and examples of how leaders who apply transformation principles achieve a unique cultural DNA for their organisations. This enables the move through the transactional processes to that of transformation. Step by step, Claudio explains that only when everyone takes ownership of the process, based on their shared values, does the organisation stand a chance of being transformed. We in South Africa understand this only too well. We have wonderful laws, structures and systems but we have not undertaken the necessary transformation process to Steward Leadership which Claudio maintains, with well-reasoned arguments, is essential to transform our society. Constantly harkening back to the vision of the organisation with people encouraged to develop their personal potential, as well as developing others in the organisation, is now the way forward. While the role of the Leader continues the expectation of providing security, he has now moved on from providing security in the cave. The new barbs and arrows are those of social media and for that a new set of skills is required. For the future, it is psychological security which is paramount - security (and wellness) in the job and in career planning. The Leader has now become a Coach whose foremost task is to develop people in the organisation. Adapting the words of Rosalind Carter, the former US First Lady (wife of former US President, Jimmy Carter), we could say that:

"The leader takes people where they want to go.

The Steward-Warrior Leader takes people where they don't necessarily want to go, but ought to."

This sounds just like the book all South African and World Leaders should be reading.

Keith Richardson
CEO of The Principals Academy Trust
Former Principal Wynberg Boys' High & Springfield Convent

Table of Contents

Note from the Author

The book encompasses a collection of leadership insights gleaned from my own bold path, frequently beyond the confines of life's 'safety net'. These insights are shared for your benefit, dear reader, as you navigate your own journey in an ever-evolving world, with new obstacles arising constantly.

There is no shortage of references in leadership literature regarding leading with vision or having ambitious dreams. However, what if all goes wrong and you miss your target? Or, if your business encounters a disruption that diminishes morale and makes the objective no longer viable?

This book also explores leading during unfavourable times, not just focusing on empowering to thrive during the favourable times, which ideally should be the leader's main emphasis. The leader must be prepared for the impending storm, while still being mindful of capitalising the sunshine. The season of summer will eventually come to an end, and winter will follow suit. Have you made preparations for it? Inspiration is drawn from lessons passed on to me by mentors and colleagues, from over two decades in the unforgiving environments of the military and corporate specialist banking. To have a better understanding of leadership, for years I waded through an ocean of books, academic research papers, theories, blogs and speeches. When reading the below extract from *The Economist,* it was evident that I was not alone.

"The sheer amount of guff written about leadership, management and careers is staggering. Publishers spew out new business titles, some good, most not. Research papers proliferate, exploring everything from the impact of Covid-19 on leadership in dental practices in England to the prevalence of psychopathy among sustainability managers.

Blogs, newsletters, podcasts, social-media posts and columns (oh my God, the columns) add to the torrent of advice. It is hard for any would-be business guru to stand out in this ocean of effluent..."

The Economist, Feb 19th, 2022

To avoid this being 'just another' leadership book or a mere opinion piece, learnings are backed up by either academic research or thousands of years of hard-fought leadership lessons.

To aid comprehension and implementation of leadership, leadership theories are presented coherently with a golden thread using a historical timeline to demonstrate their interconnection and the evolution of leadership models as humanity has progressed. A case is made for a fresh approach to leadership that takes into account the unique challenges faced by today's generation, distinct from those of the past. The proposed model is called Ownership-driven Leadership and it falls along an Ownership Continuum, ranging from a hands-off approach that empowers individuals, to a hands-on approach where the leader is focused on protecting their team during difficult times. In today's rapidly changing world, leaders can no longer rely on things falling into place 'as usual', making a warrior approach to leadership essential.

This warrior approach to leadership draws from classic principles, including the 2,500 year old source for strategy, Sun Tzu's *The Art of War*, which has been applied to business strategies for years. The application of its principles, such as strategic planning and competitor analysis, can assist in the development of effective business strategies. These principles aren't meant to glorify military leadership, but rather to serve humanity in an uncertain and volatile world. To some extent, it can be seen as humanity returning to our military origins and rediscovering ancient strategies from our hunter-gatherer ancestors. Rather revealingly, even the commonly used word 'strategy' is derived from the Greek word *strategos*, which means army general.

In the dire situation we find ourselves, we need to apply principles to effectively overcome challenges and flourish, rather than be overwhelmed by the tsunami of leadership theories in existence. This is the intention, first and foremost.

Claudio Chistè

June 13th, 2023

LET'S BEGIN THIS LEADERSHIP JOURNEY TOGETHER

Introduction

A leader's influence permeates throughout an organisation. It is this influence that can inspire and light the way in the darkest of moments.

The primary objective of this book is to provide leaders with the essential tools to establish and sustain high-performing organisations, guiding them through challenging times and towards a prosperous future. At the heart of this book is the idea that a leader's positive intention, rooted in caring, is the cornerstone for developing effective leadership skills. This book also emphasises the need to cultivate a psychologically safe environment to foster high-performance and highlights that with the right mindset and support, anyone can become a capable leader.

By presenting the Steward-Warrior Leadership model, this book offers a new perspective on leadership that can aid leaders in navigating the intricate and continuously changing business environment. Moreover, the book introduces crucial concepts like Ownership-driven Leadership, which relies on an expanded interpretation of 'Ownership' and the Ownership Continuum and a comprehensive systems approach to leadership that incorporates both variables related to the leader, as well as 'non-leader' variables within the system, as captured in the Systems Leadership Equation. The leader variable pertains to the leader, focusing on the prevention of leadership failure caused by mistakes in action and psychological barriers. These insights equip leaders with a unique approach to leadership, enabling them to be more effective and better equipped to tackle the challenges of the modern business world. Drawing on two decades of practical experience and observations, this book represents the culmination of over six years of research, longer than the average duration of a Ph.D. programme, as reminded by my academic colleagues.

The overarching aim of this book is to contribute to the advancement of knowledge that can foster innovative practices and policies, ultimately improving the quality of life and making the world a better place. This book is centered on serving as a leadership manual that provides valuable insights for years to come.

The compilation of which laid the groundwork for the establishment of the *Centre for Leadership*[1], to focus on:

- Board-level executives looking to self-improve.
- Established leaders who wish to expose themselves to new ideas.
- Highly regarded leaders who have been overlooked for senior positions, who are looking for new insights, perspectives and motivation.
- New leaders who wish to grow and tap into their potential.

Inspiration for a new leadership approach

Modern leadership literature tends to emphasise long-term growth, creativity and empowerment. However, this approach is often formulated in the context of a stable and peaceful environment. Silicon Valley investor Ben Horowitz aptly refers to this as being written for an environment suited for the 'Peacetime CEO', as opposed to the challenging environment of the 'Wartime CEO'. Horowitz is a technology entrepreneur and co-founder of the venture capital firm Andreessen Horowitz, which he founded with Marc Andreessen. By the end of 2022, the company had amassed assets worth USD 35 billion under management. Andreessen, who co-created Mosaic - the pioneering web browser that played a significant role in promoting the World Wide Web - sold the license to Microsoft in 1995 for USD 2 million. After modifying it, Microsoft later rebranded it as Internet Explorer. Subsequently, Andreessen co-founded Netscape, which was acquired by AOL for USD 4.3 billion.

---

[1] This was formed by Claudio Chiste in 2021, merging in 2023 with Bruno Bruniquel Coaching to form the Centre for Leadership and Coaching.

Present times are unpredictable and complex, with each day possibly appearing crisis-like. This places a demand upon the leader to act in order to mitigate the threat. Horowitz's notion of Peacetime CEO vs Wartime CEO is considered to be one of the most cited management think pieces of the last decade. It provides the fundamental distinction of the operating philosophy that is necessary for companies to survive, reinvent and ultimately win when macroeconomic environments shift. During periods of peace, leaders should strive to expand opportunities for their employees by encouraging creativity and contributions across a diverse range of objectives. However, Horowitz explains that "in wartime, by contrast, the company typically has a single bullet in the chamber and must, at all costs, hit the target." The organisation's survival is dependent on strict adherence and alignment to the mission. An example of a wartime leader is Steve Jobs who has a classical wartime management style. He left Apple as the CEO in 1985 during their longest period of peace, to return 12 years later with Apple close to bankruptcy, akin to a wartime scenario. On taking over as CEO he required that everyone follow the business plan he implemented. It was made clear that there was no room for individual creativity outside of this core focus. In contrast, Google, who had achieved dominance in the search engine market, fostered peacetime innovation and individual creativity. Google's '20% time' rule encouraged employees to take one full day per week to work on their own project. The rationale was that by incorporating time for play and imagination, this would serve as catalyst for creativity resulting in increased productivity. The Covid-19 pandemic spurred the debate of 'wartime vs peacetime' leadership to enter mainstream debate. In wartime, a nation could find itself fending off an imminent existential threat. This threat could come from a wide range of sources including a dramatic macro-economic change or a supply chain shortage. The words of General (retd) Wesley Clark, former Supreme Allied Commander of NATO, provide insights into the current times. During an interview on March 3, 2022, he stated:

"There is no business as usual anymore."

This is the 'new' business as usual. Although these times may be uncertain, this can be seen to exist on a continuum. At the one end of the continuum utter chaos and at the other end the new business as usual. The reality is, with the 'new' business as usual, even though there may not be an actual crisis underway, one could rapidly unfold when least expected. In light of this new reality, rather than debate whether a leader can be both a peacetime and wartime leader, the *real* question should be:

"What skills does a leader need to develop in order to lead in both peace and wartime?"

The Steward-Warrior Leadership equips leaders with tools to navigate both favourable and unfavourable circumstances using ten essential dimensions for effective leadership. This approach helps leaders develop skills to adapt, overcome obstacles and drive success.

Unpacking the concept of leadership

Before delving into these dimensions, let's clarify our concept of leadership. The book discusses leadership on three levels:

1. Leading yourself.

2. Leading people/an organisation. This is the core focus of this book.

3. Leading strategically (systems thinking, understanding context).

From my own practical experience and observations of leadership, many modern leadership models appeared to have important aspects missing. In the present times of increasing volatility and complexity, they often appear abstract and somewhat far removed from practical application. My view was further influenced by four factors. Firstly, my upbringing in Africa and exposed me to traditional African leadership perspectives. These perspectives prioritise collectivism through principles such as Ubuntu and Batho Pele, as well as the Zulu concept of leadership presence known as 'Isithunzi'. I was also inspired by classic traditional leaders like Chief Maqoma and King Moshoeshoe, who demonstrate effective leadership in turbulent times.

As a result, my outlook is grounded in empathy and compassion, while still prioritising effectiveness. Secondly, my military experience and exposure to concepts of leadership principles in current contexts, are strengthened by the works of military strategists like Sun Tzu and Carl von Clausewitz. Thirdly, my experience as an international banker during the most severe economic downturn since the *Great Depression* gave me valuable insights into an aspect of leadership that prioritises commercial and market-oriented strategies. Lastly, my academic research, initially intended for my PhD but since repurposed for this book, has contributed to my integration of established leadership models with my diverse range of learnings.

Modern leadership theories place significant emphasis on the importance of a leader's vision and motivation towards it. However, they frequently overlook crucial aspects that contribute to effective leadership, such as inspiring Ownership and providing support to ensure psychological safety. The concept of *Ownership-driven Leadership*, a term introduced in this book, encompasses these crucial aspects of leadership.

The concept of Ownership is illustrated through the use of a submarine as an example. In a submarine there are numerous controls which could impact the safety of the submarine if used in an erroneous manner. Even the most junior possibly having access to these controls. Regardless of seniority, the mission depends on everyone taking ownership of their part, with the slightest dereliction of duty by anyone impacting the safety of everyone.

The concept of Ownership

When the word 'ownership' is capitalised, it signifies a fresh perspective on this term, highlighting three crucial concepts which constitute the 'Ownership Triad', namely:

Own who you are. Own the mission. Own the result.

The concept of Ownership is broad, essentially capturing both responsibility and accountability. Although responsibility and accountability are often used interchangeably, they have distinct meanings.

Own the mission

Ownership Triad

Own who you are   Own the result

Source: © C. Chiste 2021

Responsibility vs Accountability

Responsibility refers to the duties and tasks that one is expected to carry out. Accountability, on the other hand, is the obligation and willingness to accept the consequences and outcomes resulting from the completion or non-completion of those assigned duties and tasks: Who is answerable for the outcome?

By instilling a sense of ownership, the mission can be seen as something that 'belongs' to the person assigned the task, rather than just a task to finish. David Marquet, a US Navy Submarine Commander, highlights the significance of a bottom-up emphasis empowering **team members to take ownership** of their work and decisions. According to Marquet, leaders should provide their team members with more decision-making authority and motivate them to take initiative rather than solely following orders. This results in teams becoming more engaged, motivated and productive. This is the delegation of responsibility in order to enable team members to make decisions. On the other hand, Jocko Willink, a former US Navy SEAL Commander, emphasises a distinct facet of leadership, referred to as Extreme Ownership. Even though leaders may delegate responsibilities, accountability remains with the leader. Meaning that while decision-making authority might be delegated for certain matters, the leader retains the overarching accountability to ensure the functioning of the entire system. Responsibility encompasses the requirement to execute tasks or adhere to regulations, while accountability involves being held responsible for the consequences of those tasks or processes. This approach aligns with the philosophy encapsulated by the famous phrase "the buck stops here", often attributed to US President Harry Truman.

Crucially, leading by example assumes a pivotal role. It necessitates the leader's willingness to take Ownership of mistakes or shortcomings, thereby cultivating a culture of accountability within the team. This top-down emphasis on accountability is fundamental in establishing an environment where responsibility is upheld from the highest echelons to the rest of the team. The concept of Ownership is a vital aspect for both the leader and team members. The following is an elaboration of the three components of Ownership:

1.   Own who you are

This component relates to having self-acceptance, owning both your successes and your dark side. This is enabled with continuous self-reflection.

2.   Own the mission

Have belief in both the mission and your people, inspire the same in the people for them to also own the mission and take Ownership.

"War is the realm of uncertainty; three quarters of the factors on which action in war is based are wrapped in a fog of greater or lesser uncertainty.

A sensitive and discriminating judgment is called for; a skilled intelligence to scent out the truth."

Carl von Clausewitz, from his book *Vom Kriege* (1832)

Translated into English as *On War*

General Carl von Clausewitz was a Prussian general and military theorist who was involved in numerous military campaigns. He is famous primarily as a military theorist interested in the examination of war, utilising the campaigns of Frederick the Great and Napoleon as frames of reference for his work. Clausewitz is regarded by many as one of the greatest strategic minds of all time and made the point that the implementation of a plan is seldom seamless. Surprising things could happen which differentiate reality from the plan on paper, resulting in "even the simplest thing becoming difficult".

Although he did not use the term **fog of war**, it has emerged as a popular term to characterise the confusion and uncertainty experienced during battle. The fog of war can affect anyone, in any aspect of life. Although situations may differ, everyone will experience it eventually. This can occur in your professional or personal life, shifting your focus from long-term planning to short-term tactics. During the 'fog of war', demands intensify and difficult decisions must be made to manage competing priorities. Processing information quickly can make it hard to recognise patterns to readily separate "the wood from the trees". Furthermore, stress can limit logical and creative thinking. Leaders must be capable of making split-second decisions based on partial data to navigate through this difficult situation.

This book places emphasis on the leader's mindset, highlighting the need to inspire Shared or Collective[2] Ownership as the primary objective. While this may appear as relinquishing control, the leader must also possess the ability to exercise Total Ownership when the situation demands it. This is similar to the military concept of 'Command and Control', defined by NATO as being the exercise of authority and direction by a properly designated commander over assigned forces in the accomplishment of the common goal (mission). Even if the leader passes control, Command is retained, thus preserving the right to take the control back at any time he[3] sees fit. Total Ownership can be compared to Centralised Command, when the mission or task is brought under a single, central authority. Likewise, Shared Ownership could be compared to Decentralised Command when administrative functions or powers are distributed. From an academic perspective, Centralised Command is maintaining authority while providing direction or giving orders on how to operate or function. Decentralised Command is the distribution of authoritative power to various local authorities, to allow action based on current knowledge. The military perspective essentially expands this to allow combat decisions and

---

[2] The term 'Collective' is capitalised as a proper noun since it refers to the people a leader serves and is generally preferred over 'Followers' to avoid implying a binary choice, of being a leader or follower. The view is that leadership involves both leading and following and that leaders can either be born or made. Furthermore, a good leader also needs to be a good follower.

[3] He or his can refer to male, female or any other gender identification.

actions to be made at the lowest possible level in a chain-of-command. This is based on situational knowledge, objectives, intent and local intelligence.

Providing a framework and a response plan allows for decentralised action. Each echelon knows and understands the role of the others, enabling sound decision-making. This is particularly beneficial when confronted with the fog of war when information flow becomes impractical or unreliable. It is critical that there is adequate practical training, accompanied by well-defined guidance and intent. US Navy Vice Admiral Henry Mustin stated in his fighting orders to the US Second Fleet, responsible for the East Coast and North Atlantic Ocean:

"The basic requirement of decentralized operations in general war is pre-planned response in accordance with commonly understood doctrine. Lord Nelson did not win at Trafalgar because he had a great plan, although his plan was great.

He won because his subordinate commanders thoroughly understood that plan and their place in it well in advance of planned execution. You must be prepared to take action... when certain conditions are met; you cannot anticipate minute-by-minute guidance."

3. Own the result

This component revolves around assuming responsibility, irrespective of the results. Accountability entails acknowledging one's role and duties, including decision-making. Even if there was not a unanimous consensus during the decision-making process, every individual 'owns' the result. While others may be responsible for carrying out the task, the ultimate accountability for its completion lies with the leader. In other words, the leader is the one who bears the final responsibility. Ownership can be thought of as being along a continuum, referred to as the **Ownership Continuum**. At one end of the continuum the leader has a hands-on approach (in a crisis), whereas at the other end the leader has a hands-off approach. During a crisis, the leader consolidates control to effectively address the challenge, embracing a Warrior Leadership style and assuming Total Ownership. The Collective's support for the leader's Total Ownership approach is conditional upon three things:

Firstly, trust is built during business as usual: When a leader prioritises empowering their team members during the regular course of business, trust in that leader is likely to be built up. This trust serves as a stable foundation for relationships and interactions during 'business as usual'. However, during times of crisis, uncertainty, or significant change, trust becomes even more critical as individuals and organisations face heightened levels of risk and volatility. Trust serves as a valuable asset during these situations, providing stability for relationships and interactions. Over time, the development of trust can generate a sense of security and predictability. The return on the leader's investment in his empowering approach can be seen as the **'new currency'** because it serves as a strong and reliable foundation for relationships and interactions, which can prove invaluable during times of uncertainty. Secondly, the leader is motivated by a Selfless interest: It is understood that the leader's action in response to a crisis will be solely in the best interests of the Collective. Thirdly, Total Ownership is temporary and has risk: Once the crisis is over, the leader will revert to Shared Ownership. **Taking bold action carries risks**, including the need to manage resistance, opposition and unintended consequences that can harm reputation and credibility.

The **Shared Ownership** of the Steward Leader involves empowering people, inspiring them to take on an active role in the organisation's success. This incentivises people, making them feel like stakeholders. The risk for a political leader is that disengaged, marginalised and vulnerable citizens could become the targets for opportunistic self-seeking and corrupt conspirators seeking to advance their own nefarious agenda. Steward-Warrior Leadership can be seen as inspiring people to live an Ownership-driven life that aligns with the highest level of Maslow's hierarchy, associated with purpose and self-transcendence.

Figure 1
The Ownership Continuum

Total Ownership	To Survive (crisis)	Ownership Continuum	To Flourish (non-crisis)	Shared Ownership
Task-oriented with people in mind (to solve problems/issues)				People-oriented with task in mind (directed to vision)

Source: © C. Chiste 2021

Chapter 1
The need for a NEW Leadership Model

"When the rate of change outside exceeds the rate of change inside, the end is in sight."

Jack Welch

The present-day world is marked by ever-changing realities and the emergence of new challenges. In fact, Vaclav Havel, the former President of the Czech Republic, asserted upon accepting the Philadelphia Liberty Medal that we have sound reasons to believe that we have left behind the modern era and are now entering a **'challenging new world'**.

The risks posed by these challenges are considerable, not only for leaders but also for humanity as a whole. Various theorists have put forth different interpretations of the current epoch. The three most prominent of these are Age of Globalisation, the Information Age, and VUCA times (which stands for Volatile, Unstable, Complex, and Ambiguous).

Figure 2
Challenging new world

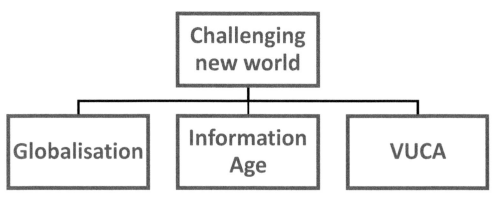

Source: © C. Chiste 2021

When taking a problem-solving approach, it is crucial to avoid showing preference for a single narrative and instead examine all three to comprehend the risks they present. Although there may be varying opinions on which narrative is the most accurate, all three are considered valid because the risks they present are real and demand our attention.

The main message conveyed by all three narratives is that the world we inhabit is undergoing a state of 'self-exhaustion' due to the long-term strain caused by human actions, including the excessive consumption of non-renewable resources, prolonged exploitation and deforestation for urbanisation. It appears as if the world we know is crumbling, decaying and exhausting itself. Whilst it seems that something is on the way out, we should be aware that there is something else painfully being born. Havel commented that there are many things that indicate that we are going through a transitional period. Although still unclear, it seems that something else is emerging from this rubble. The risk is that our way of life could be disrupted, with the 'ultimate disruption' being a threat to human existence. It appears that the possibility of this is inching closer. This is evidenced by the statement on Russia's state TV (April 15th, 2022), following the sinking of the flagship of Russia's Black Sea Fleet, the Moskva, during the Ukrainian-Russian conflict. The commentator had stated that the ongoing conflict has "**escalated into World War 3**".

We are living in a world of increasing uncertainty. This can be felt economically, environmentally, politically and in recent years also pandemically. If any confirmation is needed, a quick glance at media headlines or the antagonism and polarisation on social media is sufficient to confirm that the world we once knew is no more. These times require that leaders be resilient to withstand this unsettling turbulence. Let's take a closer look at these three challenges.

Challenge 1: A GLOBALISED WORLD

Feelings of scepticism, neutrality or apathy may arise when people don't buy into the leader or fully embrace his vision and values, potentially resulting in disconnection from the leader's stated intention. As a result, people are unlikely to be moved by the leader's call to action. The Western world has undergone significant changes in perspective, driven by factors such as increasing diversity and the emergence of Generation Z (born 1997-2012) into adulthood. This generation, the first to grow up with the internet as an integral part of daily life, has never known a world without email, instant access to information and mobile phones. This differing world view presents a new challenge for leadership. The leader who fails to be aware of the changing *zeitgeist*[4] of the Collective, is in peril of losing touch with reality. The leader will not be able to resonate with the Collective in order to tap into unifying sentiments, thus giving way to polarisation.

Figure 3
US ideological polarisation at 150-year high

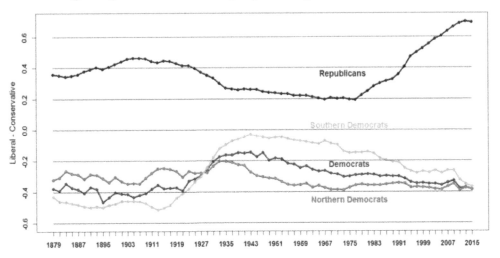

The data in the above graph shows the increasing US polarisation.

Credit: Nominal Three-step Estimation (NOMINATE). Data generated by Professor James Lo based on the analysis of voting records, survey data and cross-party affiliations.

---

4 Zeitgeist refers to the defining spirit or mood of a particular period of history, as shown by the ideas and beliefs of the time.

Using the US as an example: The last time such polarisation was seen was 150 years ago. To put this into context, that was in the aftermath of the devastating US Civil War, which tragically resulted in an estimated 750,000 deaths.

Shared values act as a unifying force, which have been compared to as glue, also acting as a compass, keeping people aligned towards the right direction. The topic of **diversity** has become increasingly controversial in recent years due to the **polarisation of values,** particularly in developed countries.

Countries from the Organisation for Economic Co-operation and Development (OECD) have high-income economies, accounting for two-thirds of World trade, 50% of both Global GDP and energy consumption (2020). Understandably, membership of the OECD is often used as the main criterion for developed country status. Thus, statistical data from OCED countries can provide insight on trends and cycles in the broader developed world. Developed countries are often seen as leading the way in terms of progress and are viewed as predictors of what is to come for the rest of the world. This progress is not limited to manufacturing and democracy but also encompassing social changes, including American pop culture and evolving attitudes towards diversity. In terms of ethnic diversity, there has been a notable increase in developed countries.

Figure 4
Foreign-born population as percentage of OECD population

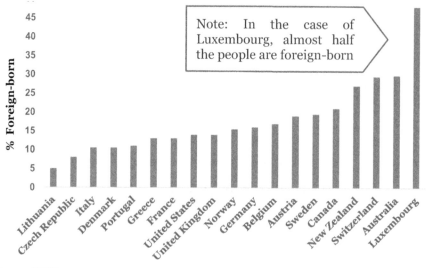

Note: In the case of Luxembourg, almost half the people are foreign-born

Source: OECD, 2019

14

We have seen the definition of **diversity** undergoing significant change in recent years, particularly within developed countries, no longer assumed to refer to ethnicity or culture. It now encompasses a range of factors such as economic status, age, gender, sexual orientation, disability etc. This too could be seen as a predictor of what is to come for the rest of the world as countries continue towards becoming developed.

Leaders in developed countries face the challenge of leading an increasingly diverse population, risking loss of national identity, shared values and unity. How can a leader cope without understanding this changing environment?

Literature provides knowledge, but comprehending the context is crucial for principles-based application. According to Russ Ackoff, a theorist of organisational studies, an era is characterised by "critical cohesiveness brought about by a common view of the world". The cornerstone of our reality is the perspective we all share, and as such, a leader should be a transforming influence who inspires a common vision, contributing to social coherence.

Challenge 2: THE INFORMATION AGE

"New sensors, from humdrum dashboard cameras to satellites, are examining the planet and its people as never before...

... States can be humbled – open-source intelligence proved that Russia shot down a Malaysian airliner over the Ukraine in 2014 and provided evidence of the scale of China's internment of the Uyghurs.

*The decentralised and egalitarian nature of **open-source intelligence erodes the power of traditional arbiters of truth and falsehood**, in particular of governments and their spies and soldiers. For those who believe that secrecy can too easily be abused by people in power, that is good news."*

The Economist, August 5th, 2021
(the power of open-source intelligence)

We are currently experiencing one of the most significant shifts in human history, characterised by unprecedented access to vast amounts of information. Despite humanity having existed for thousands of years, the last 150 years have seen more advancement in technology than all the previous years combined. Electricity, motor vehicles, plastic, cellphones and television are all inventions brought to consumers during this period. Newer innovations, such as the internet, have spurred on even more rapid societal development. Given that global economies are increasingly dependent on information, the Information Age is often used to describe the present era. However, there are other facets of the advancement being witnessed. In order to gain a broader perspective of the present era, it's necessary to examine the historical events of the preceding eras. Broadly speaking, civilization can be chronologically ordered into four phases:

Phase 1: The Age of the Hunter-gatherer

Each morning the hunter would need to rise and set off armed with bow and arrow or sticks and stones to gather food for his family.

Phase 2: The Agricultural Age (also known as the Agrarian Age)

The farmer would need to work the land, from where the adage "you reap what you sow" originates. Notwithstanding the use of oxen to plough the ground in preparation for planting the seeds, producing food was very labour-intensive. In fact, before the industrial revolution, 90% of the workforce was employed in agriculture. After harvesting, the farmer would need to plough the land again for the new planting season.

Phase 3: The Industrial Age

Many farming jobs were lost in this age due to mechanisation. However, many new jobs were created as factories were built, with productivity increasing by 50 times compared to the Agricultural Age. Years later would see jobs reduced as a consequence of delegation and scalability, with technology allowing raw materials to be taken through an assembly line with high levels of efficiency.

Phase 4: The Information Age (includes Industry 4.0)

The mid-20th century saw the ushering in of the Information Age, where the economy shifted from heavy industry to one focused on information technology. This was a consequence of significant government investments in new technologies, specifically electronics and computers, aimed at supporting the military war effort during WW2. These technologies found widespread use in the business world once the war was over. This age is evolving into the Knowledge Worker Age, or simply known as the **Knowledge Age.** Another narrative of the current times is the industry-focused Industry 4.0.

Will the next tech evolution be the next industrial revolution?

In November 2022, the Information Age reached a **new frontier** with the launch of ChatGPT. This technology can prove useful in gathering information from open-source intelligence (OSINT). While the exact definition of the Fifth Industrial Revolution (5IR) is yet to be established, it is widely accepted that 5IR builds upon Industry 4.0, also known as the Fourth Industrial Revolution (4IR), but with a fundamental difference in the technologies involved. The 4IR is generally characterised by the integration of advanced technologies like the IoT, big data, automation and AI into existing systems to enhance efficiency and productivity. In contrast, although 5IR is still a developing concept, it is believed to involve the convergence of various technologies such as AI, robotics, 3D printing, nanotechnology and biotechnology to create entirely new systems and possibilities. In other words, 5IR is about creating new technologies and systems that are not just improvements on existing ones but are fundamentally transformative in nature. To provide further context, below is a snapshot of the historical progression of previous industrial revolutions.

Manual labour/ handcrafts	First	Second	Third
	Mechanisation (steam engine)	Technical (mass production)	Digital (computers, automation)
	This period is commonly referred to as the Industrial Age.		

The technological 'final frontier': Singularity

Moore's Law states that the computing power of microchips doubles every two years. The implications of this growth in computing power extend far beyond hardware becoming more powerful. It could lead us to the final frontier of technological advancement as we know it, as computing capabilities continue to increase exponentially. What is this final frontier?

The concept of singularity is regarded as the final frontier. It is a theoretical time in the future when the progress of technology transforms human civilization: an inflection point for human-AI interactions. Singularity is a hypothetical scenario that some experts believe could be achieved within the next few decades. Futurist Ray Kurzweil predicts singularity in 2045. A graph of Moore's Law can visually represent the predicted technological advancement towards singularity. This shows computing power consistently and exponentially increasing over time.

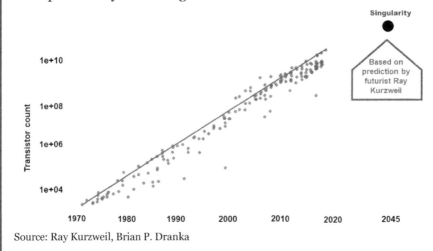

Source: Ray Kurzweil, Brian P. Dranka

Singularity could result in advanced AI technologies becoming widely integrated into society, paving the way for unprecedented levels of productivity, efficiency and innovation. However, AI development poses risks of uncontrollable outcomes that could act against human interests. AI systems with their own objectives could result in unintended consequences and catastrophic outcomes. To manage AI risk, ethical governance frameworks are needed to align AI systems with human values.

As a result of the recent technological advancements, workers can now achieve higher levels of productivity, resulting in increased economic growth. Starting from 1760, the advancement of technology in relation to human history is visually depicted by graphing the total hourly output of the UK and the USA, both considered as leading developed nations.

Figure 5
The evolution of technology and human societies:
From the printing press to the current global internet

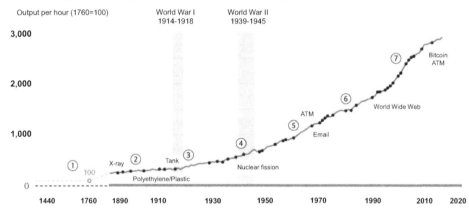

Source: Barclays

Note: The productivity in 2018 is around 3,000 on this index. Further detail on the above graph is presented below.

Figure 6
Seven periods of innovation and growth in productivity:
Expansion of figure 5

① 1890 and earlier

1440 Gutenberg Printing Press
1480 Sea astrolabe
1589 Mechanical knitting machine
1608 Telescope
1630 Slide Rule
1765 Watt's steam engine
1790 Sewing machine
1816 Telegraph
1867 Dynamite
1879 Light bulb

② 1891 -1910

1893 Diesel Engine
1895 X-ray
1898 Polyethylene/plastic
1903 Gas turbine
1909 Television broadcast

③ 1911 - 1930

1911 Cloud chamber
1915 Tank (during WW1)
1928 Penicillin

④ 1931 - 1950

1931 Electron microscope
1933 FM radio
1935 Nylon
1938 Nuclear fission
1941 Polyester
1947 Transistor
(hydraulic fracturing)
1948 Atomic clock

⑤ 1951 - 1970

1953 Video tape recorder
1956 Hard disk drive

1957 IBM 610 Sputnik 1
1960 Laser
1967 ATM (Barclays)
1970 Pocket calculator

⑥ 1971 - 1990

1971 Email Intel 4004
1972 Magnavox Odyssey
(first commercial home video game console)
1973 Capacitive touchscreen (CERN)
1975 Altair 8800
(micro-computer)
1980 Flash memory
1982 CD-ROM
1984 Cell phone
1990 World Wide Web
1990 Hubble Space Telescope

⑦ 1991 - present

1992 Text messaging
1993 Apple Newton
1993 Mosaic
(Web browser)
1995 DVD
1995 Windows 95
1996 USB Ports
1997 Netflix
1998 Google
2000 Bluetooth
2001 iPod
2003 iTunes Music
2004 Facebook
2005 YouTube
2006 Twitter
2009 Bitcoin
2013 Bitcoin ATM

Source: Barclays

*"We are living in **times of rapid change**. In this century we have advanced from the bicycle to the Concorde and explored the heavens on a manned voyage to the moon.*

The pace is fast, and 'never' is often just around the corner."

Anton Rupert, from his book *Priorities for Coexistence*

Advancements are taking place everywhere, from groundbreaking activities like space travel to routine duties, such as organising books in a library. Not long ago, the typical way to find information was to find the relevant a book in a library using the Dewey system. This had the potential to be a drawn-out process depending on the queue, but now, the typical way one would primarily search for information is to simply use a search engine on the internet. Search engine technology makes it easier for people to access information that would otherwise be scattered around the web. This characterises the Knowledge Age, where even the most junior team members can potentially have the same access to information as their superiors. Information has become democratised, and someone in a small rural village can potentially access the same information as an academic researching a thesis at a top university based in a major global financial centre.

In the Knowledge Age, leadership literature emphasises people-centric leadership, which requires different skills than the centralised approach of the Industrial Age. Leaders now face the challenge of leading in an era where information is easily accessible to everyone. Organisations that rely on a purely centralised approach, where the boss is the sole source of information, are ineffective. With access to information, remote work has become possible, and during the Covid-19 pandemic, many shifted from in-office to remote work. As restrictions eased, hybrid work emerged, posing challenges for leaders to maintain social cohesion, participation, confidentiality and trust.

Manipulation of information by anyone

The ease of access to information in present times presents a significant risk, as individuals with internet access may exploit it for malicious or political purposes, resulting in the potential for manipulation. The primary sources of information have traditionally been journalists and authentic media outlets who, to some extent, had to verify their sources and the information. However, this is unfortunately no longer the case. Furthermore, the advancement in AI has meant that fake content can be created to appear to be believable. The sophisticated AI used in doctored or artificially generated videos and photos, referred to as deepfakes have the ability to superimpose the physique and face of one person on another. The potential consequences of misusing deepfakes, such as manipulating a video to make it appear as if one world leader is insulting another world leader, could be extremely severe.

Given the ease with which false information can be generated, it is not surprising that the term 'fake news' has become a widely recognised phrase. This phrase became widely known during the 2016 US Presidential election, resulting in Collins dictionary designating it as the Word of the Year in 2017. It is described as a *"false and sometimes sensationalist information presented as fact and published and spread on the internet."* Michael Radutzky, the producer of *CBS 60 Minutes*, the oldest and most-watched newsmagazine on television, defined fake news as: *"Stories that are provably false, have enormous traction (popular appeal) in the culture, and are consumed by millions of people."*

Manipulation of information by the leader

It is worth noting that there may be situations where a leader deems manipulation acceptable if it results in a beneficial outcome. Fearmongering is a manipulative tactic that involves spreading exaggerated rumours of impending danger to induce fear and control people. The emotional response elicited by fear can disrupt the prefrontal cortex, which is responsible for rational thinking, causing individuals to cease thinking critically. Evolutionary psychology suggests that being alert to danger is an inherent instinct that has been vital for human survival over time.

There are situations in which a leader may justify the use of fear to prevent an impending danger. For instance, even after the leader attempts to create urgency by stressing the significance of implementing a change management process, individuals may still exhibit apathy or disinterest, lacking a sense of urgency to take action. However, this is a complex issue that necessitates introspection and careful consideration. By virtue of leaders being public figures, they have a duty of care as to how they influence. Leaders are encouraged to see themselves as teachers, coaches, mentors, or stewards who enable. By tapping into intangible qualities like integrity and trust, the leader builds commitment and responsibility among the Collective. It is hoped that this Information Age will gradually morph into an Age of Wisdom, with the low barrier to readily access information and knowledge making it easier for anyone to use this for the collective good.

Effective leadership encompasses not only the act of leading, but also that of following. To 'follow' entails being receptive and responsive to feedback, which necessitates attentively listening to one's surroundings and drawing learnings from life's experiences. Learning goes deeper than simply learning a particular set of functional skills or being able to demonstrate a series of competencies. Contemporary leadership literacies are closely connected to and expand upon the notion of learning. During a period of paradigm shift, the definition of learning can broaden to encompass the concepts of re-learning and un-learning.

In order to understand how the choice of leadership style could affect individuals in a knowledge-intensive economy, it is important to have knowledge of the fundamental values, assumptions and ideologies held by those individuals. The rising trend of 'cancel culture' in the Information Age is characterised by the act of 'being cancelled'. This trend operates on the notion that despite a history of positive actions, a single mistake can nullify all the positive aspects learned over the years, resulting in a negative perception that becomes the new reality of how an individual is viewed. By possessing this understanding, leadership can be guided in their social media practices.

"In a few hundred years, when the history of our time is written from a long-term perspective, it is likely that the most important event those historians will see is not technology, not the internet, not e-commerce. It is an **unprecedented change in the human condition***.*

For the first time, literally, substantial and rapidly growing numbers of **people have choices***.*

For the first time, they will have to manage themselves. And **society is totally unprepared** *for it."*

Peter Drucker
(Drucker providing clarity on the challenges we face)

Drucker's quote suggests that the most significant change that historians will recognise when reflecting on these times will not be technological advancements such as the internet or e-commerce. Instead, it will be an unprecedented shift in the human condition, where people now have more choices than ever before. This shift in the human condition requires individuals to manage themselves, taking personal responsibility for their decisions and actions. Drucker observes that society is not equipped to handle the shift, suggesting that we lack the necessary tools and systems to help individuals manage themselves effectively.

With the widespread availability of negative content on the internet and dark web, there are many harmful and tempting options that can threaten one's well-being. The content we choose can either enlighten or dumb down, so leaders should provide guidance to ensure that people make informed choices that serve their best interests. To enable people to manage themselves effectively and lead a purposeful life, it is important to inspire them. Ownership-driven Leadership can achieve this by providing safety in order to inspire empowerment through direction, guidance, mentorship and coaching.

While social media influencers have the potential to impact the minds of young impressionable minds, it is crucial to consider the content posted: Is it mindless entertainment for the sake of growing followers and making a buck? Does this entertainment run the risk of followers engaging in dangerous activities? Does the content aim to add value to a world in need of not only humour, but also direction and healing?

Society is continuing to move away from Industrial Age thinking, a time when choices were limited to the few. Broader society now has access to choices, consequently, there has been a corresponding shift towards a decentralised leadership approach to meet the needs of the time. It's crucial to acknowledge that turbulence and disruption are increasingly prevalent in today's world. The term VUCA, originally used to describe modern warfare, is now widely employed in business. This necessitates a leadership mindset that can adapt to complexity and chaos, which may appear to be at odds with the decentralised approach. Therefore, it's imperative for leaders to be flexible in their leadership style to navigate the constantly changing environment of what is known as the times of VUCA.

Challenge 3: VUCA TIMES

"Change has never been this fast and will never be this slow ever again."

Gordon Moore, Intel co-founder

Leadership models need to adopt a situational approach to effectively respond to unprecedented disruptions caused by complex issues like technological advancements, shifting power dynamics and environmental challenges. The UN intergovernmental body, the Intergovernmental Panel on Climate Change, warned of the danger to humanity's future if environmental action is not taken (February 2022), stating: "The scientific evidence is unequivocal: climate change is a threat to human well-being and the health of the planet. Any further delay in concerted global action will miss a brief and rapidly closing window to secure a livable future."

Technology dependence heightens cyber-attack risk, affecting all nations and institutions. For example, trade in South Africa's major ports grinded to a halt in July 2021, causing a severe negative impact on container shipping supply chains. The South African Transnet Port Terminals (TPT) division reported this disruption incident as "an act of cyber-attack, security intrusion and sabotage". The TPT declared *force majeure* at South Africa's major shipping terminals, namely the ports of Durban, Ngqura, Gqeberha (Port Elizabeth) and Cape Town.

Furthermore, technological advancements, such as online ordering, has enabled commerce to be delivered straight to the consumer, rather than following the conventional approach where the consumer visits the marketplace. This has negatively impacted the wholesaler and retailer. This is known as disintermediation, which effectively shortens the supply chain by creating a direct interaction between the manufacturer and the buyer, i.e. the reduction in the use of intermediaries between producers and consumers. An example of this would be investing in the securities market directly, rather than through a bank.

The diagram below shows that week-on-week volatility from recent times is comparable to that of the 1930s-40s, which were marked by extreme events like the *Great Depression* and WW2.

Figure 7

Market volatility in recent times resembles levels of WW2: Week-on-week percentage change in S&P 500

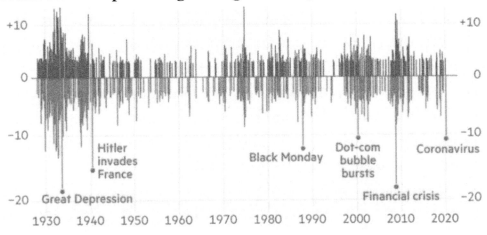

Source: Refinitiv, Financial Times

A year after the onset of the Covid-19 pandemic the *Deloitte Global Resilience Report* found 60% of C-suite executives were of the view that disruptions would be a regular occurrence in the future. Meaning that the disruption experienced during the Covid-19 pandemic is merely the start of more to come. The market volatility evidenced is in the context of an interconnected world.

Whilst studying at the South African Military Academy, the concept of **complex interdependence** was emphasised. This term was popularised by Robert Keohane and Joseph Nye in the 1970s and used to describe the dependent nature of the global political economy. It can be seen as applying a **systems thinking** approach to nation states, with both the direct and indirect knock-on effects to be considered. Complex interdependence describes a situation in which multiple actors, such as states, organisations and individuals, are mutually dependent on each other in a complex and interconnected way. In such a system, the use of force or coercion is limited, and cooperation and negotiation are more effective means of achieving goals. This mutual dependence emphasises the importance of multiple channels of communication and interdependence in international relations, rather than a traditional view of power relations based solely on military or economic strength.

In recent years the concept of complex interdependence has evolved in relation to the growing importance of information and communication technologies (ICTs). The rise of ICTs has enabled greater interconnectedness and interdependence among actors in different domains, such as politics, economics, and society. This change occurred during the late 20th century and early 21st century, as the internet and other ICTs became increasingly pervasive and transformative. Keohane and Nye revisited this concept (1998) to emphasise information flow, citing a notable increase in '**information interdependence**' within the global environment.

The most uncertainty in recent times

In January 2023, the Doomsday Clock was moved 90 seconds to midnight: the **closest it has ever been to a global catastrophe**.

The clock represents how close the world is to disaster, with the minute hand showing how many minutes until midnight, the **metaphorical end of the world.** The Bulletin of the Atomic Scientists (BAS), with input from its Board of Sponsors including Nobel laureates and experts, decide to move the Clock closer or farther from midnight. The Clock was initially used to represent the danger posed by nuclear weapons, though in recent years includes climate change, bio-threats and disinformation. The inclusion of disinformation reflects its potential to undermine responses to global catastrophes by eroding public trust and creating confusion particularly through fake news. This makes coordinated responses to existential threats more challenging, contributing to the potential for a catastrophe.

The BAS was founded in 1947 by prominent scientists, including Albert Einstein and those who were involved in the development of the world's first atomic weapons as part of the Manhattan Project. Given their experience and expertise, if anyone had knowledge of the perils confronting the world, it would be them.

Today's leaders face mounting difficulties presented by Globalisation, the Information Age and the VUCA environment. To confront these challenges, leaders need the ability to tap into a warrior mentality and philosophy that is fit for adversity. Warriors are defenders who safeguard their people and way of life from harm. The model proposed in this book highlights the importance of stewardship and leading through service, integrating these values are at the heart of the Steward-Warrior Leadership Model. This approach offers a fresh viewpoint on contemporary leadership. The purpose of this model is to merge established leadership approaches, creating an effective leadership style that enhances, rather than replaces, existing knowledge and expertise in leadership.

Caveat: Going back to the age-old debate as to whether leaders are born or made, for our purposes this does not matter. Leadership can either be innate or acquired and even those who possess natural leadership abilities can still benefit from self-improvement. Only a decade or so ago, being assisted by an executive coach may have been seen as a sign of weakness, possibly even seen as remedial education. A signal that help was needed to overcome a challenge, because you were incapable of resolving it on your own. According to the International Coach Federation (2019), the situation is undergoing a change as the expenditure on executive coaching worldwide has reached USD 2.85 billion. Executive coaching is increasingly being likened to that of a sports coach honing the performance of an elite athlete. It is rare to find an elite athlete who does not have a coach.

However, self-reflection is crucial for maintaining a high level of self-actualisation. It is important to note that this leadership model may not be suitable for everyone, particularly those who prioritise their self-interests and are unwilling to engage in honest self-reflection. It requires a unique type of leader who is called to serve.

It's time for new dimensions to be added to existing models.

As we get older, our needs invariably change. Similarly, as our society and world changes, new needs and new threats emerge. As the needs of the times have changed through the ages, leadership models have had to adapt accordingly. Rather than regarding one model better than the other, each model should be considered in the context it was developed, with due regard to the peculiarities of that context. Regardless of how good a model may have been deemed at a point in time, history shows that there comes a time when a model needs to adapt. Today we are seeing the world we know changing before our eyes. It is time to add additional dimensions to existing leadership models to keep up with this change. To begin exploring how leadership has evolved over time, let's start by examining early models of leadership.

Timeline of leadership model evolution

Classical mythology is filled with great hero-leaders who slew terrifying monsters and battled fearsome enemy armies.

Among the most well-known is the epic poem of ancient Greece, *The Odyssey*, attributed to Homer. This is estimated to be dated between 675 and 752 BC. Along with *Iliad*, these two epic poems are regarded as the foundational works of ancient Greek literature. In those times, leadership was based on the view that impact was made by the individual leader alone. *The Odyssey* is the epic tale of Odysseus, the King of Ithaca, who undergoes a 10-year struggle to return home after the Trojan War. During these years he often single-handedly battles mystical creatures and has to deal with the wrath of the gods.

Another example is *Beowulf*, regarded as the highest achievement of Old English literature and the earliest European vernacular epic. The poem is believed to have been composed between 700 and 750 AD. It describes how a young Swedish prince, Beowulf, cleanses the town of the evil monster, Grendel. The hero-leader Beowulf exhibits great bravery in everything he does.

The Epic of Gilgamesh, considered the **oldest written poem in existence**, serves as another illustration. Although not as famous as other examples, it was penned over 4,000 years ago, pre-dating the renowned works of Homer by nearly 1,500 years. Gilgamesh was the King of Uruk in Mesopotamia, described by the historian Samuel Noah Kramer as follows:

"Gilgamesh became the hero par excellence of the ancient world—an adventurous, brave, but tragic figure symbolizing man's vain but endless drive for fame, glory, and immortality." In the eyes of the Ancient Mesopotamians, a hero was an individual possessing exceptional courage and bravery, capable of rising above ordinary people.

These earlier views of hero-leaders have become known as the **Great Man theory.** This theory dominated discussions on leadership prior to 1900. The basic tenet of this theory was that great leaders are born not made.

In the early 20th century, the **Trait Theory of Leadership** was introduced which asserted that leaders can be born or made. This theory refers to the general characteristics of a leader, including capabilities, motives and behaviours. It does not make an assumption as to whether leadership traits were inherited or acquired, simply asserting that the characteristics of a leader are different to those of non-leaders. Consequently, researchers tried to identify the traits of great leaders in terms of physical, mental and personality traits. It was found that there are certain traits which theorists associate with great leaders. The focus generally tended to be on certain leadership traits, namely: determination, intelligence, self-confidence, integrity and sociability. Nonetheless, there are numerous other traits which can be considered such as vision, discernment, courage, humility, honesty, empathy, loyalty, commitment, competence, inspiring others and problem-solving ability. In fact, Bass (1990) identified 43 distinct traits, stating that the significant number of traits without a unifying personality framework posed comparison challenges.

However, a prevailing view on personality's structure emerged from factor analysis which revealed five main personality factors, often remembered with the acronym OCEAN: Openness (to experience), Conscientiousness (achievement orientation and dependability), Extraversion (sociability and dominance), Agreeableness (trusting, cooperative, caring, and tolerant) and Neuroticism (emotional instability). These five traits are often used as predictors across different domains in industrial-organisational psychology, including job performance (Barrick & Mount, 1991). According to Judge, Bono, Ilies, and Gerhardt (2002) there is a positive correlation between openness, conscientiousness, extraversion and emotional stability and leadership. Due to a shift away from physical demands in the modern era, leadership theories that emphasised masculine traits, like the Great Man theory and early Trait Theory, have lost much of their relevance. Critics contend that Trait Theory focuses solely on leader's traits, neglecting other crucial factors. While theorists agree traits alone don't guarantee success, a leader's situational response is vital, giving rise to behaviorist psychology.

Behavioural leadership theories indicate that the group's preferred leadership style is influenced by its nature and challenges. Further research supports leadership as a phenomenon affected by circumstances or context. Rather than try to figure out who effective leaders are and what their traits are, i.e. the WHO of leadership), the focus shifted to behavioural theory, specifically to determine what effective leaders do. This focused on how leaders obtain their results and the process they followed, i.e. the HOW of leadership. Modern leadership theorists generally agree that traits alone are not an effective way to explain leadership. More recent theories of leadership have tended to explore leadership behaviour in the context of the situation and the people involved.

Fiedler's **Contingency Theory of Leadership** (1964) states that leadership effectiveness depends on matching the leadership style to the situation. The theory assumes that there is no single best leadership style and that the style is fixed and natural for the leader, which differs from modern theories.

To determine a leader's natural leadership style, the **Least Preferred Co-worker (LPC) model** explored many factors, including the relations with the leader and the task structure. A high LPC score meant a relationship-orientated leader, whereas a low LPC meant a task-orientated leader. Hersey and Blanchard's **Situational Leadership** theory introduced in 1969 gained popularity in the 1980s and is still popular today. This theory suggests that leadership style is not fixed, with a leader being able to change between relationship and task focus depending on the situation. The extent of this orientation between relationship and task behaviours being dependent on the maturity of the followers.

The **Path-Goal theory** introduced by Robert House in 1971 affirmed that the traditional method of characterising a leader as either highly participative and supportive or highly directive is invalid. It was concluded that leadership behaviour may vary to address subordinate satisfaction and motivation. The role that **Emotional Intelligence (EQ)**[5] plays in leadership performance gained

---

[5] Although Goleman is credited with the term Emotional Intelligence, it was first used by graduate student Wayne L. Payne in his doctoral dissertation in 1985. It later appeared in academic research in 1990, when two university professors, John Mayer and Peter Salovey, conducted research to measure the difference between

prominence through Daniel Goleman's writings (1995). He defined EQ as the array of skills and characteristics that drive leadership performance in different situations. Most elements of emotional intelligence models fit with four generic domains, namely: self-awareness, self-management, social awareness (empathy) and relationship management (social skills). The examples of leadership theories covered above are by no means complete. The intention is to merely illustrate the different approaches taken over the years. What these theories illustrate is that to be successful, leaders must be concerned with both task-related and people-related issues.

While **Servant Leadership** may be a timeless concept, the actual term was only coined in a 1970 essay by Robert K. Greenleaf, in which he wrote:

"The servant-leader is a servant first... It begins with the natural feeling that one wants to serve, to serve first.

Then conscious choice brings one to aspire to lead. That person is sharply different from one who is leader first, perhaps because of the need to assuage an unusual power drive or to acquire material possessions... The leader-first and the servant-first are two extreme types. Between them there are shadings and blends that are part of the infinite variety of human nature."

An expansion of Servant Leadership is that of **Steward Leadership**, which also emphasises the concept of stewardship. Peter Block, the author of *Community: The Structure of Belonging*, defines stewardship as:

*"The willingness to be held **accountable** for the well-being of the larger organization by operating in service, rather than control, of those around us."*

---

a person's abilities in and around the emotions. This term was made famous after Oprah and Dr Phil used their platforms to showcase Goleman's work. In fact, the origins of this concept date back further to 400BC, with Socrates's injunction 'Know thyself' speaking to the keystone of emotional intelligence: self-awareness.

The concept of the Servant and Steward Leader, with the leader being a servant first, is well entrenched in Africa. The South African term **Batho Pele** (Sotho-Tswana) translates as *People First*. This concept was first formally introduced by the Mandela Administration in 1997, to serve as a reminder that government leadership stands for being of service to the public. It is important to understand that Batho Pele is not a plan or a strategy, rather it is an attitude that shapes the character of the public service. It serves as a reminder that the citizens are the reason why public service exists in the first place. The principles include the following:

- Consult: Consult with citizens to understand needs and expectations.
- Set service standards: Establish and adhere to service standards to ensure consistent and quality service delivery.
- Be accessible: Be accessible to all citizens, regardless of their location, economic status, or physical ability.
- Be courteous: Treat citizens with respect and dignity at all times.
- Provide information: Citizens have a right to be informed about the services provided by the government.
- Practice openness and transparency: Be open and transparent about decision-making processes, policies and actions.
- Redress issues: Citizens have a right to complain and seek redress if they are not satisfied with the services provided.

A fine example of a Servant and Steward Leader is King Moshoeshoe I (1786-1870), who was well-known for his acts of friendship, even towards his enemies. An instance of such diplomacy was noted by Robert Mangaliso Sobukwe, founder of the Pan Africanist Congress (PAC), in the book by Benjamin Pogrund, *How Can Man Die Better*. After Moshoeshoe triumphed over Mzilikazi, a former general of the Zulu under King Shaka, he demonstrated exceptional kindness. As Mzilikazi's defeated warriors withdrew, Moshoeshoe showed compassion by sending a large herd of cattle to his 'brothers' to ensure that they had sustenance for their journey home. Mzilikazi never attacked him again.

Moshoeshoe's reputation for diplomacy extended beyond showing mercy to his defeated foes. He generously granted land to impoverished tribes and imparted them with the knowledge and skills to cultivate their crops. According to the book *History of the Basuto: Ancient and Modern* by D.F. Ellenberger (1861), the cannibals of the present-day Lesotho once numbered 4,000. These numbers were put into context when Ellenberger estimated that each

Classical **Servant and Steward Leader**: King Moshoeshoe was well-known for welcoming refugees and victims of the Mfecane/Difaqane wars into his tribe.

cannibal could potentially eat a minimum of one person a month, thus a minimum of 48,000 people may have been eaten annually. From the period 1822-1828, this would equate to a staggering 288,000 people being eaten. Despite the fact that the cannibals had committed the horrific act of eating his grandfather, Peete, Moshoeshoe still displayed compassion towards them. He lured them out of their cave with raw meat and successfully negotiated for peace. Furthermore, he supported their rehabilitation by teaching them agriculture, enabling them to live off the land.

The concept of stewardship

The essence of stewardship lies in fostering people's abilities and a favourable environment to enable empowerment. According to the Merriam-Webster dictionary, the term steward is formally defined as the careful and responsible management of something entrusted to one's care.

Dr Kent R. Wilson argued in his PhD thesis for the expansion of the definition of stewardship, in order to fully express what it means. This expanded definition sees stewardship not only being the **management or caring** of other people's property or resources but expanding this to include **human resources and potential**. Stewardship can be seen as a force multiplier, amplifying effort to produce more output.

It is apparent that during times of prosperity, leadership may not seem to matter, with people having short-term focus on the pleasures of life or the next dopamine hit from social media. During dark times of hardship, such as when business owners encounter financial difficulties or when violence and looting breaks out, leadership can become a matter of literal life or death.

Amidst challenging times, leaders must embrace the Warrior Ethos, which involves demonstrating a deep sense of responsibility towards their team while exhibiting a fighting spirit and prioritising the achievement of goals over personal gain. In essence, this means that the Warrior Leader must have the willingness to courageously lead in order to serve the greater good through selfless action. This is 'Courageous Selfless Action'.

Having played a crucial role in the Frontier Wars, Chief Maqoma (*Jongumsobomvu*) is recognised as one of the most exceptional military leaders in 19th-century Africa and a classic example of a Warrior Leader. Maqoma was the Right-Hand Son of King Ngqika, ruler of the Xhosa nation's Rharhabe Kingdom. According to Xhosa oral tradition, Maqoma earned the nickname 'the Leopard of Fordyce' for his role in leading the Waterkloof battles, during which the highest-ranking British officer was killed, Lieutenant Colonel John Fordyce.

The battle for Waterkloof in the Amatola Mountains in 1851 is considered Maqoma's greatest victory. This battle formed part of the Eighth Frontier War (1850-1853). These battles, amongst which includes the battle to relieve Governor Sir Harry Smith, who was trapped in Fort Cox by the Xhosa, are amongst the biggest battles ever recorded in South Africa.

Classical **Warrior Leader**:

Chief Maqoma undertook Courageous Selfless Action to serve the Collective.

Credit: National Heritage Monument

According to the historian Rob Speirs, who specialises in battle tours along the Eastern Cape, up until the 2nd Anglo-Boer War the battles of the Eighth Frontier War were the most protracted in history. In fact, up until the Battle of Isandlwana they accounted for the highest death toll in history. A comment from contemporary chief and descendent, Chief Island Siqithi Maqoma, adds perspective when he stated:

"Small wonder that the Eastern Cape has more forts than any other place in Africa.

This is because it was here that the British fought longest and hardest..."

The Steward-Warrior Leader arises as a result of combining the distinct leadership styles of the Steward and the Warrior. This approach reflects the idea of leaders who are called upon to serve selflessly, prioritising the empowerment of the Collective, whilst demonstrating courage and boldness in their actions. A modern-day example of such a leader being Madiba. The name Madiba is a traditional clan name used to refer to Mandela as a sign of respect. Those who had the privilege of being around Mandela frequently remark on his remarkable talent for making them feel seen, heard, and loved, thus instilling in them a feeling that they mattered. Nevertheless, the leader must also be ready to take bold action. This may require him to make difficult and unpopular decisions during moments of crisis. Steward-Warrior Leadership can be defined as follows:

Modern-day **Steward-Warrior Leader**:

As president, Mandela practiced Steward Leadership putting the needs of the Collective first, focusing on reconciliation and creating opportunities. During his time as a 'freedom fighter', he exemplified Warrior Leadership, taking Courageous Selfless Action, which ultimately resulted in 27 years imprisonment.

"The ability to forge together a diverse grouping of people towards a shared vision creating social cohesiveness, a sense of Ownership, safety and trust in the leader.

In times of adversity, the trust built up in times of 'business as usual' enables the leader to selflessly take on challenges with the backing of the Collective."

Leading interconnectedly[6] like Madiba

Systems thinking aids the leader whether to use a hands-on or hands-off approach. It recognises that an organisation is made up of various interconnected parts, with a change in one part having a ripple effect throughout the system. By understanding this interconnectedness, the leader is more likely to take a hands-on approach in times of crisis, intervening in the system to prevent or mitigate negative consequences. For example, during a major shift in the market or a disruptive event, a leader may need to be more directive and hands-on in his approach, providing clear instructions and guidance to their team to navigate the situation. This allows the leader to take charge and make critical decisions to help steer the organisation through the turbulence. Conversely, during more stable times, a leader who understands systems thinking may adopt a hands-off approach, empowering his team to make decisions and take Ownership. By doing so, the leader creates an environment that fosters innovation and encourages the team to think critically and solve problems collectively.

It can be said that **interconnectedness** concerns both **systems thinking** and the philosophy of **Ubuntu**, as it extends to collaborating with people to work together towards a common goal. Mandela's Madiba Magic enabled him to connect with people, a combination of charm, charisma and authenticity that allowed him to bridge divides and bring people together. One of the ways he did this was by making an effort to speak with people in their own language and to understand their culture and interests. While he was imprisoned on Robben Island, Mandela learned to speak Afrikaans, the language of his jailers, as a way to communicate with them and build rapport. He also took an interest in rugby, a sport then seen as a symbol of Afrikaner identity. This broke down barriers and built relationships that would later serve him well in his political career.

---

[6] Leading interconnectedly refers both to systems and people. It means being aware of the interconnectedness of different parts of a system and how they affect each other and using this understanding to guide decision-making and actions as a leader. Leading interconnectedly also involves collaborating with others and building partnerships across different parts of the system to create mutually beneficial solutions.

He also had a long-term perspective and believed in addressing the root cause rather than just the symptoms. This informed his systems approach, using both hands-on and hands-off strategies as appropriate to the situation. This is the essence of *"leading 'interconnectedly' like Madiba."* Examples systems thinking applied to determine leadership approach:

Hands-on approach: An example is when he negotiated the end of apartheid with the South African government. Mandela recognised that the situation called for a decisive and direct approach. He engaged in direct negotiations and was actively involved in shaping the negotiations, sometimes through difficult and confrontational discussions. Mandela was able to navigate these challenges and eventually reach an agreement that brought an end to apartheid.

Hands-off approach: Mandela also used a hands-off approach when he established the Truth and Reconciliation Commission (TRC). The Commission was created to help heal the wounds of apartheid by investigating human rights violations and offering amnesty to those who confessed to their crimes. He did not take an active role in the Commission's work, instead empowering the commissioners to work independently with minimal interference. This hands-off approach allowed the Commission to carry out its work effectively and impartially.

Combination approach: An example of Mandela's use of both approaches was his approach to education reform. He recognised that education was a fundamental component of a healthy society and launched initiatives to improve access to education. However, he also recognised that systemic change was needed to address the root causes of educational inequality. To achieve this, he established a task force to investigate and make recommendations on how to reform the education system. Mandela played a hands-on role in shaping the task force's recommendations and was actively involved in implementing the resulting reforms, but he also empowered the task force to work independently, allowing reform implementation with minimal interference.

In the past, the mental image of a leader was often associated with a hero-figure standing triumphantly over a vanquished evil villain. This is rooted in the origin of the noun 'leader', which can be traced back to the Old English word *lædere*, meaning "the one who leads". However, the verb form lædan reveals an historically less emphasised aspect of leadership, which involves "guiding and bringing forth". This sheds light on the notion of leadership as a form of service, not the vanquishing of an evil villain. In the past century, there has been a significant shift in perspective towards the idea of a leader as both a servant and a steward. Leaders prioritising guidance and empowerment foster trust among people. As people get to know the leader, they may pose several questions concerning the leader's trustworthiness, such as:

- Do I really buy into the leader as a person?
- Am I prepared to stand by the leader even in trying times?
- Is the leader focused on self-interest or a special interest group?
- More importantly, does the leader have my best interests at heart?

The reality is that not all leaders prioritise the interests of their followers. Various factors can drive people to seek leadership roles, and some may resort to unethical methods to attain such positions. These unethical means include:

- Nepotism
- Funding from unsavoury donors and sources
- Political connections
- Playing political games
- Manipulating the news (be it the formal media or social media)
- Using populist rhetoric to stir emotions.

While a self-serving individual may hold a leadership position, he should not be regarded as a true leader. The leader needs to prioritise the interests of the people above self-interest, making time to self-reflect and focus on ways to improve effectiveness. This book starts with leadership in its 'pure' form, by incorporating learnings from our hunter-gatherer ancestors.

In those days, tribes lived in proximity to their leader, with the people knowing his every movement in both professional and personal life. Consequently, the leader would need to practice **Authentic Leadership** and have a high level of self-awareness.

The subsistence way of life and typical seasonal migratory movement of the tribe, often through harsh conditions required **Agile Leadership**. This agility ensured the leader's ability to adapt to an ever-changing and uncertain environment, ensuring the safety of the tribe.

Notwithstanding the passage of time, the one constant in the history of humankind is that regardless of the age we live in, there are times when the leader will have to make what is called the 'big decision'. In business, this is the moment where everything is on the line, with the CEO having the final say in the decision-making. Making the wrong decision could mean the end of the company, with people losing their jobs. Conversely, this decision could propel the company to an improved profitable future. In these moments, the leader takes a centralised, warrior approach, to ensure the safety of the organisation.

The Warrior Leader 'leading the way'

Credit: National Heritage Monument, King Shaka statue

Warrior Leader Women

While the warriors portrayed in this book are male, reflecting the deeply ingrained warrior-leader archetype within the South African culture, it is important to note that the same principles can also apply to women. The traits and qualities of a great warrior are not gender-specific and women have long played integral roles in battles and conflicts throughout history.

In the early days of Ancient Greece, both the Spartans and Athenians trained women in the art of war. Women were also encouraged to participate in competitive war games. In fact, the freedom of young unmarried women of the military city-state Sparta resulted in the Athenian playwright, Euripedes writing:

The daughters of Sparta are never at home!
They mingle with the young men in wrestling matches,
their clothes cast off, their hips all naked.
It's shameful!

Warrior Queen:

Nzinga has become a historical figure in Angola and in the wider Atlantic Creole culture.

She is remembered for her intelligence, her political and diplomatic wisdom, and her brilliant military tactics.

She fought for the independence and stature of her kingdoms in a reign which lasted 37 years.

Credit: Achille Devéria (artist)

Through sport these women were deliberately hardened to increase their strength, physical ability and endurance for military service. Plato states in *The Republic* that women should be allowed to become soldiers, if they so wished. Roman theorists concurred, with the philosopher Musonius Rufus (AD30-c.101) that men and women should receive the same education and training. Any difference should be based on strength and ability, not gender.

Interestingly, the only way for Spartan men to be entitled to a gravestone for their burial, was if they died in battle. Similarly, for a woman to die during childbirth was one of the greatest honours. This was seen as a duty to Sparta rewarded with a personalised gravestone.

Chapter 2
The WHO of Leadership

We all have needs that require fulfilment. The overall positioning of these needs on the hierarchy is associated with a particular level of consciousness. It's important to recognise that people may be at different points in their personal development, regardless of where they fall on this hierarchy. The leader who is able to raise his level of consciousness is able to transcend beyond the Self. This leader is called to serve for unselfish reasons. The adaptation of Maslow's hierarchy of needs presented below has an enhanced emphasis of 'going within' as graphically represented in the figure below.

Figure 8
Moving up the hierarchy

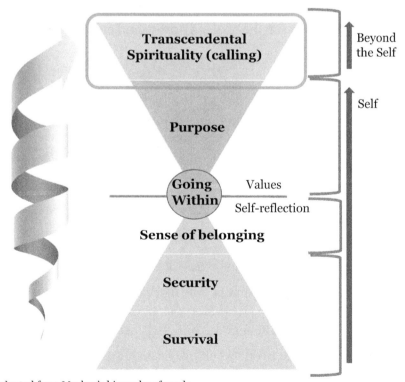

Adapted from Maslow's hierarchy of needs

Source: © C. Chiste 2021

Level 1 and 2: Survival and Security (physiological)

Survival is a basic human instinct that is mainly centered around fulfilling essential physiological needs such as obtaining food, water, and shelter to sustain life. In addition, sleep and physical fitness are also important in addressing physiological needs. Research from the University of Dundee supports this, as studies have shown that major decisions should not be made on an empty stomach. When given the option to receive a reward now or wait to receive double the reward in the future, people were willing to wait up to 35 days. However, this timeframe dropped to as little as three days when hungry. Meeting the need to survive is paramount, as it serves as a foundational human need that must be fulfilled before focusing on higher-order needs.

Level 3: Sense of Belonging (psychological)

While we may have evolved over time, many of our needs remain unfulfilled. In the days of our hunter-gatherer ancestors, people knew their leaders intimately. There was little difference between the leader's private and public life.

However, from the small, family-like tribes of the hunter-gatherer, we have moved on to large bureaucratic organisations. The Covid-19 pandemic has accelerated the globally mobile nature of the workforce as more people pivoted to working remotely. The organisations of today often do not deliver the sense of tribal belonging that people instinctively require.

Early day family-like tribe

Artist: Charles R. Knight (1874–1953) dated 1920

Servant Leadership seeks to fill this gap by building a sense of social identity and addressing the innate tribal need to belong. Teams are created to promote the close relationships that were once found in hunter-gatherer societies. In these teams, colleagues assist and help build each other's capacity. This is a leadership approach that can deal with challenges of the modern workplace.

Organisations that have implemented Servant Leadership practices attest to its effectiveness; these include the following:

- Starbucks: The employee benefits offered by Starbucks align with the principles of Servant Leadership. The benefits provided, such as health benefits, retirement savings plans and tuition reimbursement, demonstrate a commitment to serving employees and recognising their contributions to the company's success. Additionally, the parental leave policy and partner perks program show a commitment to supporting employees' well-being both in and outside of work.

- Whole Foods Market: The employee benefits offered by Whole Foods, such as health benefits, retirement savings plans, education benefits and parental leave, align with the principles of Servant Leadership. Servant Leadership prioritises the well-being of employees, emphasising their growth and development. The benefits provided demonstrate a commitment to serving employees, recognising their contributions to the company's success and supporting their overall well-being.

- TDIndustries: TDIndustries provides a range of benefits to its employees, including health insurance, retirement savings plan, paid time off, employee assistance program, life and disability insurance, employee development and wellness programmes. These benefits align with the principles of Servant Leadership by prioritising the well-being and development of employees. By providing comprehensive benefits, TDIndustries demonstrates a commitment to serving its employees and fostering a positive work environment.

These are some examples of the many organisations that have made a conscious effort to change their focus from the conventional pre-Information Age, to one that emphasises service and empowerment. Prioritising the needs of the people to ensure the organisation's long-term survival and success is of utmost importance. However, achieving it can be a frustrating endeavor, often resulting in poor management of human resources that could have been better empowered and developed.

Research from Gallup, the global analytics and advisory firm, reveals that only one in 10 people possess the inherent talent to manage, with a further two in 10 having only the basic managerial talent to be able to function at a high level, i.e. **70% of people lack management skills** to operate at a high level. This suggests that a high percentage of teams will have a manager who falls into this unfavorable category. According to Hogan, a specialist in personality assessment and leadership development, 80% of people experience job-related stress, of which **75% link this to their boss.** According to the American Psychological Association, stress results in accidents, absenteeism, decreased productivity, employee turnover, increased direct medical expenses and legal costs. US firms incur a cost of USD 300 billion yearly on stress impacts.

Before technology, leadership was mainly a physical activity. In those days, the primary determinant of survival was supremacy in the hunt or in hand-to-hand combat, this characterised the Great Man Theory. As a result, natural selection was likely based on physical traits. However, today physical strength is generally no longer a requirement. Furthermore, given the intimate nature of the small hunter-gatherer tribes, leaders had to lead by example and often from the front Nowadays, many leaders lead from the back: the US President leads from the Oval Office, while during the battles in Ukraine, President Putin was not seen personally leading any charges from a tank. Even big tech founders such as Bill Gates wield power from a keyboard, without physical strength.

Filling the literature gap to present the full leadership picture

Leadership is an omnipresent characteristic of human society that impacts everybody's life. As a result, it is an inescapable topic that draws diverse perspectives. Studies have shown that people possess an innate ability to recognise leadership qualities upon encountering them. However, the subject of effective leadership remains a highly debated issue within the realm of social sciences, encompassing both an art and a science. Despite the extensive literature available, there is no commonly accepted comprehensive method on how to integrate or complement models. There could be several reasons for this, but the following four shortfalls in the literature are worth mentioning.

Shortfall 1: Non integrative and complementary approach

Leadership academic theories are often presented in **silos**, which limits their relevance to the real world and creates a cluttered understanding.

To address this shortfall, this model integrates popular models to bring clarity to the complex landscape of leadership, including aspects of Authentic Leadership, Trait Theory, Situational Leadership, Emotional Intelligence, Transactional and Transformational Leadership. Critical interdisciplinary thinking breaks down silos, allowing theories to complement each other and add unique pieces to the puzzle, resulting in a more comprehensive understanding. Models are generally developed in response to a lesson learned or to address a contemporary need. In this sense, it is a model of that particular context. Identifying the golden thread of how they all add a piece to the puzzle, acknowledges that each piece is valuable to the overall understanding of the puzzle. This enables leaders to apply the related theory in a practical manner. Sadly, leadership application has been negatively influenced by Niccolò Machiavelli. He asserted that in times of adversity, "It is better to be feared than loved, if you cannot be both. But one should avoid being hated." This idea has influenced leaders who have sought to maintain their power and control through fear, intimidation and manipulation. However, it is important to note that this approach to leadership can be problematic from an ethical standpoint and can lead to abusive and exploitative behaviour towards followers, stakeholders and competitors. Effective leadership should prioritise ethical considerations and strive for a balance between achieving goals and treating others with dignity and respect. To not get lost in all the detail, this model maintains that the leader's **selfless intention** serves as the ultimate driving force. Caring is

Selfless intention: Leadership starts with caring. The leader must have a good heart, i.e. this is **Batho Pele**, with the intention being to put the People First. This is the leader's why.

the foundation of all other aspects of leadership. Even if a leader has charisma or a good reputation, they cannot be considered a genuine leader without a selfless intention.

Shortfall 2: The imprecise definition of proximate leadership

Research on **proximate leadership** - the degree of leadership closeness and visibility - reveals a complex concept with multiple factors and variables.

To fill this gap, this model emphasises proximate leadership that focuses on building relationships. Although it is not usually expressed directly, at its essence, it relates to the degree of resonance with the leaders. Unfortunately, people in leadership positions are often seen as living in a parallel universe, creating a sense of disconnect and reducing their relatability to those they lead. For example, there is a phenomenon prevalent amongst some politicians disparagingly referred to as the 'blue light brigade'. Blue-light convoys with blaring sirens provide priority in traffic for VIPs. Performing this practice outside of emergencies jeopardises driver safety and raises questions about these politicians' awareness of everyday citizen struggles. Relationship-building is enabled by establishing **rapport**. Leaders who engage in active listening and support can foster an environment in which their selfless intentions are apparent to others. Stephen Covey suggests that active listening involves seeking to understand before being understood, requiring attentively listening with empathy to fully comprehend the message being conveyed. This enables the leader's intention to resonate with people, strengthening trust in the authenticity of the professed intention. Drawing inspiration from Madiba, this approach encourages people to feel seen, heard and valued. This cultivates a culture that prioritises empathy and fosters a **sense of belonging** and **connection**.

This selfless intention needs to be seen for people to believe in the leader's goodwill. This builds rapport and trust. People must see that the leader has a good heart, i.e. **Ubuntu** emphasises 'seeing' the interconnectedness of all humanity, highlighting compassion and community. This draws parallels to the Zulu phrase 'ndiyakubona', meaning "I see you" (Afrikaans "Ek sien jou"), translating as leader's 'perceived why' and the Sanskrit *Namaste*, "my Higher Self greets your Higher Self".

Shortfall 3: Leadership often focuses only on the leader

Although leadership models differ, they share a commonality: focus on the leader's approach as being critical to achieving effectiveness. However, there are a number of variables which could impact the leader's ability to lead. For example, leaders with exceptional skills could have their effectiveness undermined by deliberate acts of sabotage. In these cases, success is not solely dependent on the leader's abilities, highlighting the impact of external circumstances. Another example relates to group decision-making. Groupthink allows for information sharing but can be dangerous if the need for consensus overrides critical thinking. Factors such as conformity pressure, self-censorship or an assumption of unanimous agreement can cause intelligent individuals to make poor decisions. Thus, it's important to avoid extreme viewpoints while remaining mindful of the potential hazards.

To overcome this shortfall, the Servant Leadership model places emphasis on the importance of carrying out due regard to **systems thinking** while applying the HOW of leadership, as this systems approach encompasses other non-leader variables that can impact leadership effectiveness. These

The focus is primarily on the leader applying the HOW of leadership (the ten dimensions). However, systems thinking is also necessary to consider non-leader variables. The leader can apply the ten leadership dimensions with the best intention, yet the effectiveness may be hampered by variables in the broader system. The ability to lead with a systems thinking approach while collaborating with people as an extension of the system can be described as **"leading interconnectedly like Madiba"**.

variables could be within the organisational system (the enlarged container covered in Chapter 6) or external to the organisation. These non-leader variables encompass effective communication, the people involved, the organisation's culture and the extent to which individuals feel psychologically safe within the organisation (covered in Chapter 7).

Shortfall 4: Leadership often from a western perspective

Although leadership is widely considered a universal phenomenon, its operationalisation is often seen as culturally specific. There are conflicting perspectives in the leadership literature regarding the transferability of specific leader behaviours and processes across cultures.

For example, House, Wright, and Aditya (1997) highlight the perception among Arabs that leaders are worshipped as long as they hold power. In Malaysian culture, leaders are expected to display humility, modesty and dignity. In the US, there is appreciation for two types of leaders: those who empower and delegate authority to subordinates and those who possess boldness, confidence and a willingness to take risks, akin to the cowboy persona of John Wayne. In European contexts, leadership is often viewed as an unintended and undesirable consequence of democracy (Graumann and Moscovici, 1986). On the other hand, Indians prefer leaders who exhibit nurturing qualities, dependability, sacrifice, authority, and strict discipline (Sinha, 1995).

It is important to note that many of the prevalent leadership theories and the empirical evidence supporting them are predominantly influenced by American or European perspectives. These theories tend to emphasise individualistic, hedonistic and rational values, while downplaying collectivist, altruistic, and religious values prevalent in other cultures (House et al., 1997).

This discrepancy highlights the need for greater recognition and inclusion of diverse cultural perspectives in leadership literature. By embracing a more inclusive approach, we can better understand and appreciate the cultural nuances that shape leadership dynamics, leading to more comprehensive and relevant theories and practices. This book addresses this with the inclusion of South African concepts such as **Batho Pele**, **Ubuntu**, **Isithunzi** directed towards the goal intended to be attained, referred to in Zulu as the ***injongo***.

Learning from our ancestors

Leadership models have evolved over millennia to meet changing human needs, with styles continuously adapting since the dawn of humanity. To gain a deeper insight into this evolution, let's trace back to the early days of human existence. According to Yuval Noah Harari, the author of Sapiens: A Brief History of Mankind, even though humans dominate the Earth today, 70,000 years ago, humans were relatively insignificant in comparison to animals. In considering the difference between a human and any other animal, comparisons are often centred around intellect or even physical attributes.

Interestingly, on a one-on-one basis, humans are surprisingly similar to chimpanzees. In fact, according to the American Museum of Natural History we share 98.8% of the same DNA. However, the key difference is on the collective level. Despite cultural differences, humans share substantial cultural universals. Since the time of our hunter-gatherer forebears, human conduct has been shaped by a sustained process of adaptation aimed at meeting basic human

As Nigel Nicholson of the London Business School frames it:

"You can take the man out of the cave, but you can't take the cave out of the man."

Credit: Bryant, William Cullen, 1794-1878 Gay, Sydney Howard, 1814-1888. Contributing Library: Lincoln Financial Foundation Collection

needs in a continuously shifting environment. Although fundamental human needs remain unchanged, the means of meeting them are constantly evolving in response to changing contexts. Abraham Lincoln summed this up when he stated, *"Human action can be modified to some extent, but human nature cannot be changed."* By studying our ancestral heritage, we can understand the enduring principles that have allowed humanity to survive over time. Throughout history, humans have demonstrated remarkable creativity and resilience in devising practices and cultural behaviour that fulfills the fundamental need for survival.

51

"Culture eats Strategy for breakfast."

Peter Drucker

Drucker's statement aligns with Clausewitz's assertion that the "**best strategy is always to be very strong**; first in general, and then at the decisive point." An organisation's strength is demonstrated by its response during the critical moments of a crisis, known as the 'decisive point'. This response is often characterised by mantras such as "when the going gets tough, the tough keep going", which highlight the nature of what is required to succeed in such situations. However, the strength of an organisation is also measured by routine activities, behaviour and the conduct of its people during normal operations. Daily cultural behaviour plays a crucial role in determining an organisation's success and even conversations between individuals can significantly influence culture. Research suggests that healthy conversations can improve organisational culture by increasing engagement and collaboration, reducing stress and burnout, improving decision-making and enhancing creativity and innovation. By promoting a culture of healthy communication, organisations can create a positive and productive work environment that benefits both the employees and the organisation as a whole. A **healthy culture** is often considered more important than implementing a well-crafted strategy, as the saying goes, "culture eats strategy for breakfast."

Culture can be by design or by default. Regardless of the strategies and processes in place, an organisation's culture holds the power to empower or disempower. For successful strategy implementation, a strong culture with clearly defined values and mission is critical. A positive culture can motivate employees to collaborate towards shared objectives and make decisions that align with company goals. During difficult times, a robust culture unites individuals to confront challenges together. Conversely, a weak culture can result in unproductive outcomes.

Blanchard identifies three key components that foster culture:

- A well-defined vision
- Definite values
- Explicit internal goals (aligned with the vision).

Culture can be defined in many ways. Prof Geert Hofstede defined culture as:

"It is the collective programming of the mind that distinguishes the members of one group or category of people from others."

African cultures are recognised for their collectivist nature, which is founded on a framework of extended family and community. In these cultures, individuals prioritise the objectives and norms of their in-groups, be it family, tribe or nation. This inclination towards in-group values is a significant factor that shapes group behaviour. On the contrary, in an individualist culture, people tend to prioritise personal goals and individual achievement over that of their in-group.

To change this requires 'culture-shaping', which is a practice that typically demands a long-term strategy. To establish a certain behaviour as a customary way of life, leaders should exert their influence on the organisation's culture during normal operations. During a crisis, behavioural changes tend to occur out of necessity rather than choice and are often accompanied by significant psychological strain and stress. Thus, a leader's perspective on culture-shaping may be influenced by past crisis lessons or potential future risks, potentially leading them to prioritise risk management and crisis prevention over the creation of a values-driven culture that inspires people and drives organisational success. However, an effective leader should strive to strike a balance between managing risks and fostering a positive culture that encourages innovation, collaboration and growth. By prioritising both risk management and culture-shaping, a leader can create a resilient and successful organisation that is equipped to navigate challenges and capitalise on opportunities.

The Culture Continuum

Prof Sumantra Ghosal uses "**the smell of the place**" as a metaphor for culture. Just as physical places have distinct smells, organisations and communities have a unique cultural essence. This essence, a combination of values, beliefs, norms and practices, defines and shapes the organisation or community. Understanding cultural dynamics is crucial for leaders to create effective transformations. The smell of the place provides insights into the underlying cultural factors that influence behaviours and decision-making processes. It represents the values, beliefs and practices that shape identity and functioning. Culture can be viewed as a continuum that ranges from a healthy culture, which generates high-performing teams, to a toxic culture, which results in poor team performance.

Figure 9
Culture Continuum:
Healthy vs Toxic Culture

Culture Continuum	
Healthy ⟵	⟶ Unhealthy (Toxic)
Productive	**Unproductive**
• High level of trust (the Warrior Ethos being the epitome)	• Infighting
• Shared beliefs	• Drama
• Shared interests	• Abuse
• Shared vision	• Immoral and illegal
• Shared values	behaviour

Source: Adapted from Dr Timothy Clark, C. Chiste 2022

The Culture Continuum depicted above illustrates the key factors that contribute to a healthy culture. These positive factors are made possible through the leader's transformative influence, which will be further explored in the third leadership dimension. In contrast, a toxic culture can have detrimental effects on individuals and the organisation as a whole. Positive cultural factors can increase productivity, as explained below.

Positive factor 1: Trust

The presence of trust creates a psychological state in which individuals are willing to show vulnerability. Such an environment promotes open communication and empowers individuals to act without fear, resulting in collaboration and teamwork. Trust in the leader is rooted in the positive expectation of his intention and the ability to deliver on those intentions, whilst adhering to effective leadership principles. At the core of this commitment is the prioritisation of the interests of the Collective, which fosters a sense of connectedness with the leader.

In the military, the high level of trust expected and required is captured by the **Warrior Ethos**. To gain a complete understanding of the central principle of this ethos, it is essential to perceive it as the ultimate manifestation of the warrior spirit. It is defined by the capacity to muster the necessary strength to conquer obstacles, particularly those that jeopardise survival, such as life-threatening situations. This is coupled with a willingness to prioritise the interests of both the organisation and its people over one's own self-interest in order to achieve the mission (the Warrior Ethos is covered in detail in Chapter 5). Meaning that if someone is willing to pay the ultimate sacrifice with their life in order to protect you, this high level of trust signifies an unwavering loyalty and devotion that cannot be easily broken or undermined. It represents the **pinnacle of trust**, where one person is willing to make the ultimate sacrifice for another, demonstrating a profound sense of honour, duty and selflessness. While such an extreme level of sacrifice is not typically required or expected in the workplace, the principle of having each other's backs is crucial in creating a culture of trust and accountability, where individuals feel safe to take risks and learn from mistakes without fear of blame or retribution. This concept of having a no-blame culture is fundamental to fostering a positive and collaborative work environment, where everyone is encouraged to speak up, share ideas and work together towards common goals.

Positive factor 2: Shared beliefs

Tradition is commonly defined as the passing down of customs and beliefs from generation to generation. Although the original significance of a tradition may become obscured over time, the continued practice of it can still have a positive impact by serving to create social bonds among people. Encouraging young people to engage in cultural activities provides them with a positive and productive way to channel their energies, while simultaneously contributing to the strengthening of society. Traditional activities, which are associated with enjoyment rather than effort, can be a powerful tool for preserving cultural heritage and ensuring that it continues to thrive for future generations. Events such as festivals or sports can serve as powerful tools for building and reinforcing a sense of community and cultural identity, while also providing a means to resist the impact of external forces such as globalisation that can threaten to erode these cultural foundations. One example is the Ganesh festivals in India, which were used to maintain Indian cultural identity during British occupation. In order to make an impact as a leader, it is crucial to possess a deep understanding of human behaviour and the values that individuals hold. This understanding provides insights into people's habitual thinking patterns. To navigate the complexities of leadership across different cultures, it's essential for leaders to cultivate cultural awareness. This helps leaders better understand human behaviour and interpret leadership behaviour in different cultural contexts, bridging the gap between theory and practice. Kurt Lewin, one of the pioneers of social psychology, summed this up as:

"Nothing is as practical as a good theory."

Positive factor 3: Shared interests

By assuming shared responsibility for their actions and sharing an interest in the nation's prosperity, individuals can work towards a common goal. JF Kennedy famously said, *"Ask not what your country can do for you, ask what you can do for your country."* This reminds us that collective responsibility is not a new concept in modern times. Shared interests could also be in the economic sense whether through property ownership, consumer bonds or a sense of access to the country's resources.

Positive factor 4: Shared Vision

When a group of individuals have a shared vision, it allows them to collaborate effectively towards achieving a shared goal. This entails people proactively supporting each other and committing to the assigned task. As a result, there is alignment of values to support this shared vision.

Positive factor 5: Shared Values

Values lie at the upper end of the hierarchy of needs. Shared values help inform and guide behaviour towards the shared vision. The Leader-Follower model, which was prevalent during the Industrial Age, poses a challenge as it fails to foster independent thinking. However, this Ownership-driven Leadership model instills a sense of purpose, enabling people to develop their own ideas.

As a result, people become more aware of their behaviour, recognising the importance of their actions in accomplishing the mission. This is demonstrated through behaviour, whether formal or informal, that shapes the organisation's culture. Despite what an organisation perceives its culture to be, true culture emerges when the leader is not present. Culture influences informal decisions made on a daily basis and how people behave when facing pressure. It is a direct reflection of the group's thinking. In order to dive deeper into the concept of culture, it is worthwhile to first provide an explanation of the notion of congruency. According to the psychologist Carl Rogers, congruence refers to the alignment of one's three Selfs, namely: the True, Actual (self-image) and Ideal Self. It is possible for the three selfs to be perfectly aligned, but it is rare. When the True Self is in alignment with the Ideal Self, and a person has an accurate and positive self-image, this translates as high levels of self-esteem, self-acceptance and congruence. In other words, thoughts, feelings and behaviours are all in harmony. However, it is common for people to experience incongruence between their True, Actual and Ideal Self. This can result in inner conflict, low self-esteem and an inaccurate perception of themselves. Therefore, the goal of going within is to achieve congruence and a healthy sense of Self.

Meanwhile, Jung posits that the Self represents the integration of consciousness and unconsciousness in an individual, representing the entirety of the psyche. Jung proposed that each person has a Self which is central to being. However, most of the Self lies hidden in the subconscious. It contains the information which we tend not to access. This is where all values, beliefs and perceptions specific to the individual lie. We often hear the words character and persona used as if they are the same thing, but they are not. The Jungian term persona is often compared to self-image, a kind of mask that we use to protect us from the outer world. The True Self can be compared to one's character. It represents your deep-rooted belief system (moral and ethical values). Although you can change your mask to hide your character, your True Self does not change. It is this True Self which British writer Stephen Fry had in mind when he said:

"You are who you are when nobody's watching."

The Actual Self, commonly referred to as your persona, is necessary to serve as a protective filter. However, to attain authentic self-expression, this filter should not serve as a mask, disguising your True Self. To provide a clearer explanation, let us delve deeper into the notion of the True, Actual and Ideal Self.

Figure 10
The Self of the individual: The concept of the three Selfs

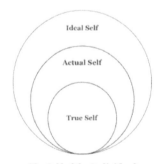

The Self of the Individual
Source: Carl Rogers

The three Selfs may not align perfectly, but it's important to let some of your True Self shine through. The filter thickness should vary with the level of trust with the person you're interacting with. As trust increases, the filter should thin, in order to reveal more of your True Self. Novelist W. Somerset Maugham contextualised the distinction between the True and Actual Self when he said:

"When you choose your friends, don't be short-changed by choosing personality over character."

To facilitate our understanding of an organisation, we can view it as a living entity like an individual. When applied to an organisation, the three Selfs concept takes on a new significance. To assist with conceptualisation, the following comparison was devised for leadership workshops I conducted, by building on the concept of the three Selfs of an individual.

Figure 11
The Self of the individual vs the Self of the organisation:
A different perspective of Culture

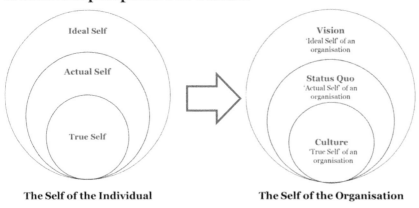

The Self of the Individual   The Self of the Organisation

Source: Adapted by C. Chiste 2021

Note: The status quo can be defined as the current state or situation of things at a specific moment in time. In the case of an organisation, this may be interpreted as its physical or conceptual existence and how it is perceived. This can be gauged based on various key performance indicators, such as brand image and profitability.

Leadership usually involves influencing self-serving individuals to co-operate towards goals. These goals are not random. They are in response to environmental demands, chief among them being survival. The evolutionary view of leadership is that it is a functional resource to ensure survival. Survival remains a fundamental human need from ancient times to the present.

Level 4: Going within (psychological): Understanding your values and self-reflection

Levels 1 and 2 highlighted the close relationship between Survival and Security and basic physical survival needs. Level 3 pertained to the sense of belonging. Research suggests that individuals who have robust social bonds tend to enjoy a longer and healthier lifespan, underscoring the significance of human connections and having a sense of belonging.

By going within, this adaptation expands the meaning of Level 4 beyond its usual association with self-esteem, instead encouraging individuals to delve into their mindset before taking on leadership positions. This includes gaining a deeper understanding of oneself beyond self-esteem, including values, motivations, thought patterns, insecurities and triggers.

A powerful way of going within is to self-reflect through meditation. Self-reflection is an ongoing process, regardless of one's level of consciousness. During a process of deep meditation whilst in a workshop, I was led to adapt Napoleon Hill's Positive Mental Attitude (PMA) to Positive Mental Impact (PMI). This is relevant for the leader to self-reflect on his leadership intention.

The question the leader could ask himself during self-reflection: Am I holding the space sufficiently to provide a sense of safety and positively influencing the people with empowerment and a sense of Ownership? From a scale of one to ten, what is my PMI?

Level 5: Purpose (psychological)

Within your set of values, there exists a hierarchy where each individual value is associated with a corresponding need. Your driving values are the values which motivate you to get out of bed on a cold winter morning. These are linked to your why. Once you reach the top of Maslow's pyramid, your focus can now shift beyond. This is analogous to shifting beyond the Self, in order to serve something greater than yourself.

Level 6: Transcendental Spirituality (calling)

This is the calling to serve. For those who have a calling to serve humanity, there is a sense of duty to be of service to others. This leader understands that it is a privilege to lead others, also understanding that leading is first and foremost about service. Service is generally viewed as something rendered to the less fortunate, the crisis-stricken and the unhappy. The thinking is that, by doing good deeds, we are making the world a better place. As Alice Bailey and the Tibetan Master, Djwhal Khul, point out in the book *Serving Humanity*, by helping others, you are primarily helping yourself without realising it. You offer help because you yourself are uncomfortable with distressing conditions which may exist. You therefore endeavour to improve those conditions, so that you feel comfortable again. Not everyone has a calling to service. Be aware that there will come a time that a threat or challenge will inevitably arise for you or your community. This may be so severe that it requires you to evoke the necessary fighting spirit. It is impossible to predict the threat which you may one day face. Irrespective of your genetics or belief system, you can tap into this fighting spirit energy. The starting point for the leader is: Own who you are. Continuous self-reflection is necessary to ensure that you keep your dark side in check. Even if self-actualisation has been achieved, a trigger could still activate your dark side. This could derail you as a leader or trigger you into survival mode. In this sense, being in survival mode is not restricted to those struggling to meet their physiological needs of food, water and shelter. The leader then engenders this amongst the Collective, leading them up Maslow's pyramid.

The ever-present risk of a downward spiral

Regardless of your position on the hierarchy of needs, a disruption could strike at any time. This could result in you having to re-prioritise your needs. For example, the *Great Lockdown* of 2020 impacted everyone to some degree, regardless of their social status. Research conducted by the National Science Foundation, an independent agency of the US government, found that 80% of people's thoughts are negative. This means that there is the risk that you may be triggered into survival mode no matter where you are on Maslow's hierarchy of needs. Negative thoughts are our default setting and have served to ensure survival of humankind since the days of the hunter-gatherer. Are you conscious of your negative thought patterns? How do these serve you?

The current times present real demands. The leader who fails to meet his own fundamental needs, regardless of whether these unmet needs are actual or perceived, is prone to being triggered into **survival mode**. This carries the risk that an entirely harmless and benign encounter may be perceived as a threat. This could also result in the justification of unethical behaviour. The diagram below shows the thought process of a trigger event.

Figure 12
Threat-reward thought processing

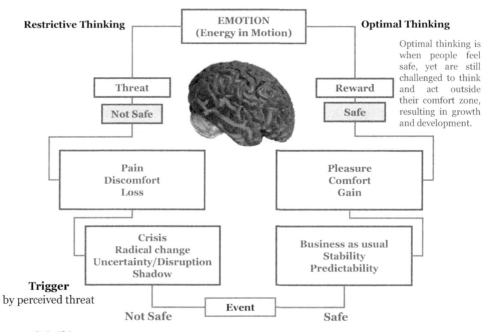

Source: © C. Chiste 2022

It's important for the leader to recognise that individuals may enter a survival mode even in the absence of physical danger. This could occur if fundamental needs are not met, such as the need to belong and self-esteem. Fostering self-reflection can increase awareness. Each level of Maslow's hierarchy has a corresponding Shadow version, indicating that even those at the highest levels of the hierarchy are at risk of having associated Shadows (Chapter 6 elaborates on this concept further). We all have a Shadow, a part of our psychological make-up that we try to deny, suppress or hide from the world.

Figure 13

The Actualised Self vs the Unactualised Self (Shadow Self)

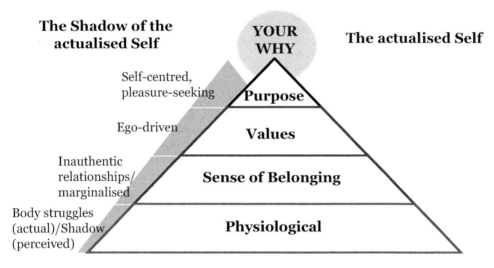

Derived from Maslow's hierarchy of needs

Note: There exists an unactualised dark side at every level, which can appear as a shadow of the actualised self. Irrespective of a leader's hierarchical position, there is always a risk that he may display self-centered behaviour. When evaluating the physiological level, it is important to acknowledge both perceived and actual unmet needs. For instance, even if someone has enough access to food and water, a scarcity mentality might result in an obsession over the accumulation of resources. Any unfulfilled need can trigger negative consequences, impacting other needs. By achieving self-actualisation, individuals can shift their focus to serving a purpose and enhancing the lives of others. A lack of purpose could result in a life defined by directionless self-centred actions, such as pleasure-seeking behaviour. An example being George Best, the legendary Northern Irish footballer, who once famously said, "I spent a lot of money on booze, birds, and fast cars. The rest I just squandered." Sadly, his undirected pursuit of pleasure, characterised by an extravagant lifestyle and alcoholism, eventually resulted in the loss of most of his fortune.

Chapter 3
The WHAT of Leadership

This chapter focuses on the **WHAT** of leadership, concerning what the leader intends to achieve. For the Steward-Warrior Leader, this is not only about leading people towards the vision, but also empowering and providing safety.

Frédéric Laloux, author of *Reinventing Organizations*, describes the Collective as a single living organism. Despite being composed of many individuals, the Collective can be seen as a unified entity with its own needs, hopes, aspirations (vision), mood (zeitgeist), concerns, fears, values and corresponding level of consciousness. An organisation's needs can be seen to exist on the Collective level, a comparison with an individual is presented below.

Figure 14
Hierarchy of needs:
The individual vs the Collective

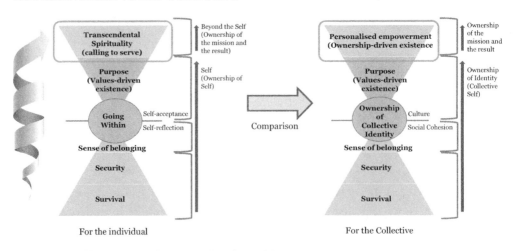

Source: Adapted from Maslow's hierarchy of needs, C. Chiste 2022

The relationship between Maslow's hierarchy of needs and levels of consciousness is such that, when the needs of individuals are fulfilled, they can advance to higher **levels of consciousness**. For example, once physiological and safety needs are met, individuals seek higher needs such as love, belonging, self-esteem and self-actualisation. Those who reach self-actualisation may experience transcendence, regarded as the highest level of consciousness.

Figure 15
Raising the Consciousness whilst leading towards the vision

The Steward-Warrior Leader leads towards the vision whilst paying attention to the needs of the Collective.

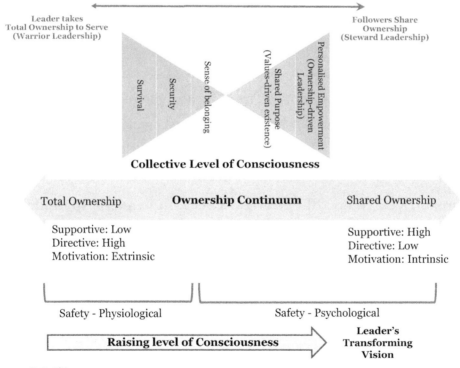

Source: © C. Chiste 2021

The above figure illustrates how the Ownership Continuum contributes to fulfilling human needs, ultimately aiding in raising consciousness. The core focus of the Steward Leader is to be of service through empowerment, as depicted by Patterson's original Servant Leadership Model (2003) to follow.

Figure 16
Patterson's original Servant Leadership model

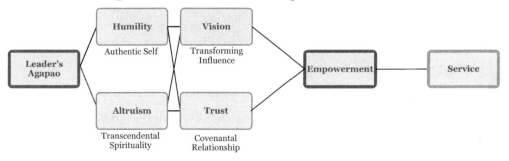

The Greek word *agapao* denotes a selfless kind of love that prioritises the well-being of others. This differs from the friendly love of *philia*. → *Agapao* is the verb-form of love, whereas *Agape* is the noun-form.

Napoléon Bonaparte rather cynically believed people are driven by either fear or self-interest, but Servant Leadership offers a third motivator: the leader's genuine caring for his people based on *Agapao*.

Winston's (2003) extension of Patterson's model showed how the behaviour of the followers, in turn, benefits both the leader and organisation. Both the leader and follower components combine to form a cyclical behaviourial pattern.

Figure 17
Winston's extension of Patterson's Servant Leadership model

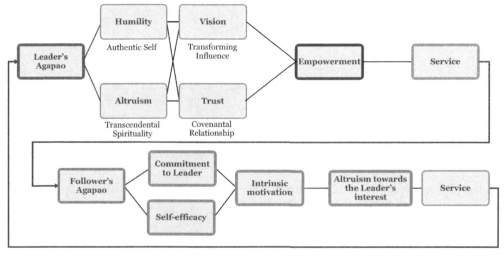

This cyclic pattern generates an ever-growing sense of commitment, expressed as service by the leader and the followers alike.

In essence, the Steward-Warrior Leadership model expands on Winston's extension of Patterson's Servant Leadership model, incorporating two crucial additions. The first pertains to seeing safety along a continuum to determine whether it is business as usual or a crisis, this provides a framework for the leader's next steps. The second addition emphasises the importance of connectedness, rooted in the basic human need for a sense of belonging, integrating the ideas of Ubuntu and Batho Pele.

Figure 18
Chiste's extension of Winston's and Patterson's model

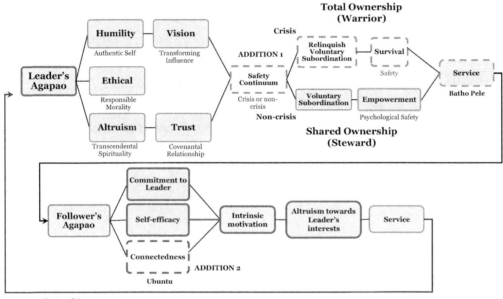

Source: © C. Chiste 2022

The two additions in the diagram above shows "Chiste's expansion of Winston's extension of Patterson's Servant Leadership model", explained below.

Addition 1: Gauging the sense of safety of the Collective (crisis vs non-crisis).

The first addition is the provision of a **framework** for leaders whether business as usual or a crisis situation, facilitated by utilising the Safety Continuum (presented in Chapter 7). The leader who views his organisation as a living organism understands the significance of ensuring a sense of safety to address the needs of their team. To illustrate this, consider a runner working to reach the finish line as a leader striving towards a vision.

During the journey, the runner may need to rehydrate to meet their physiological needs, and their morale will likely improve upon seeing intermittent signs indicating the remaining distance. These milestones provide comfort indicating that the finish line is within reach, serving to address psychological needs of assurance (certainty, security).

In times of crisis: Total Ownership

For the leader to ensure safety in times of crisis courageous action will likely be required. It is critical that this is selfless in nature, for which continued self-reflection is to be observed. This is the domain of the Warrior Leader.

In times of business as usual: Shared Ownership

During normal business operations, individuals perceive themselves as stakeholders in the organisation, exhibiting Shared Ownership. The Steward Leader assumes the responsibility of guiding people towards elevating their awareness and achieving their full potential, with an emphasis on social cohesion. The second crucial addition involves incorporating the notion of connectedness.

Addition 2: The sense of connectedness amongst the Collective.

Among the key components of a Steward Leader is inclusive leadership, by having a sense of identity through the cultivation of a spirit of **Ubuntu**. This is a well-known concept in South Africa, understood to be centred around a sense of being human. It is often simplified as *"I am, because you are."* A deeper understanding can be drawn from the Zulu phrase *"Umuntu ngumuntu ngabantu",* meaning that a person is a person through other people. A similar phrase to Ubuntu is, *"inkosi, inkosi ngabantu bayo",* meaning that a chief *is* because of his subjects. A corrupt chief would be regarded as a serious breach of mutual trust, breaking the Covenantal Relationship. Ubuntu traces its origins to the idea of serving and fostering a sense of connectedness through a community.

In recent years, the concept of **Ubuntu Leadership** has become widely recognised worldwide, with the late Archbishop Tutu particularly renowned for advocating for an Ubuntu ethic to assess South African society. He deserves significant recognition for promoting the term's popularity. However, it is to be considered an important building block for leadership, rather than a leadership style in its own right. It resonates strongly with the community-orientated approach of collectivist cultures. These cultures emphasise the needs and goals of the Collective, over the needs and desires of each individual. Ubuntu can be regarded as a manifestation of humaneness, achieved through the ability to display empathy, compassion, and mutual respect, with the goal of creating and upholding communities that prioritise justice and reciprocal care. An increasing amount of scientific evidence indicates that, akin to any other skill, compassion can be both innate and be learned. Through instruction and practical training, the skill of compassion can be enhanced. Therefore, by means of training and coaching, leadership competencies and attributes can be developed while concurrently enhancing the capacity for compassion.

Using functional magnetic resonance imaging (fMRI), the study assessed alterations in brain responses before and after training. Participants were presented with distressing images, such as a weeping child or an individual with severe burns, while inside the MRI scanner. They were then instructed to generate feelings of compassion towards these individuals utilising their acquired skills. The control group was subjected to the same images but were asked to reframe them in a more optimistic light, such as through reappraisal. The researchers gauged the degree of brain activity alteration from the beginning to the end of the training and discovered that individuals who displayed the most altruistic behaviour after receiving compassion training had the most significant changes in their brain activity when viewing images of human suffering. The inferior parietal cortex, a region associated with empathy and comprehending others, displayed heightened activity.

Note: The focus of the leader's service is to prioritise the people first, guided by the principle of **Batho Pele**.

"We are not thinking machines that feel,
we are feeling machines that think."

Daniel Kahneman, Nobel Laureate

By recognising that individuals are feeling machines that think, political leaders can develop a more empathetic and people-centric approach to service delivery, which aligns with the principles of Batho Pele. These principles emphasise the right to high-quality services and compassionate treatment. Achieving these principles depends on establishing human connections and a sense of belonging, as it results in individuals trusting political leaders and engaging more effectively. The desire for human connection and the need to belong are fundamental needs that exist in all social groups. Human connection is unpredictable and can happen unexpectedly through interactions between individuals in various situations, including crises and tragedies. These situations can bring people together to form new bonds and connections.

A real-life example of how human connection can develop unexpectedly is the encounter between former German Chancellor Angela Merkel and a young Palestinian refugee girl named Reem Sahwil. During a town hall meeting in 2015, the girl burst into tears while expressing her fears about being deported, and Merkel was visibly moved by her story. Merkel comforted her and explained that not all refugees could stay in Germany.

The emotional connection that Merkel formed with the young girl had a significant impact on the U-turn decision regarding refugees in Germany. The decision to open Germany's borders to refugees was influenced by this unexpected human connection. Ultimately, this decision resulted in more than a million refugees registering in Germany.

On the other hand, it is crucial to be mindful of the concept of 'othering', which represents the opposite of human connection. It is essential to remain vigilant about this concept because it goes against the values of human connection.

The action of othering involves focusing on differences in order to alienate, rather than unite. This prevents genuine dialogue and paves the way for discrimination and persecution. An extreme outcome of othering could be that a group of people are dehumanised, with their right to exist being questioned. An example is given by holocaust survivor, Paul Herczeg, who recalled the precise moment he was made to feel fundamentally different. Shortly after the Nazis invaded Hungary in 1944, an edict was issued that every Jew had to wear a yellow star. Herczeg added that this was the first time he realised he was different, even amongst his friends. The process of othering is driven by people categorising a group of people according to perceived differences. These differences could be in the form of inherent or acquired diversity.

Inherent diversity refers to a characteristic that a person is born into, such as ethnicity, race, religion, national origin, assigned gender or cultural identity.

Acquired or learned diversity refers to characteristics that a person has acquired after birth, such as education, citizenship, religious beliefs or socio-economic status. Learned diversity is often heavily influenced during childhood development. However, these are ultimately aspects that people can change, and often do over the course of their lives.

Many leadership models follow the Task-focus vs People-focus rationale. However, this model differs: being prepared to lead selflessly, through caring for and prioritising the interests of the people, is the only precondition. Consequently, there is no Task vs People debate, as the task is for the people. It is always about the people. This type of leader invokes a form of **providential leadership**, believing in the ultimate intention of caring and having faith that a divine energy guides events through higher forces. Despite the leader's honourable intentions, they may need to continuously motivate the Collective and foster a sense of Ownership to complete tasks, allowing for self-actualisation and expanding consciousness. As trust in the leader is built over time, the Collective begins to share a sense of Ownership and buy into the vision, feeling like stakeholders alongside the leader.

This alignment encourages the development of potential and results in the empowerment of the Collective.

In times of turbulence, the leader should avoid panicking and instead seek counsel from advisors. They should not jump to conclusions or assume a crisis when faced with unexpected challenges.

Beware of the Pseudo Transformational Leader

However, despite the effectiveness of the Transformational Leader there is a caveat. Colonel Mark Homig of the US Air Force points out that when Transformational Leadership is not authentic, it can be a 'double-edged sword'. The risk is ever present that inherent defects in personality could transform the leader into what Bass referred to as the Pseudo Transformational Leader.

According to Homig, Pseudo Transformational Leadership possesses the possibility of an immoral and unethical aspect that could be manipulated by an

unprincipled leader, causing harm to unsuspecting followers. One illustration of this is Idi Amin, who was initially regarded as a competent leader on a global scale, but subsequently earned the moniker of the Butcher of Uganda for his oppressive and ruthless regime as Uganda's President. Therefore, we see that although these dictators may have appeared to be transforming for many, their actual impact was negative. Pseudo-Transformational Leaders lacks concern for independent

Idi Amin in typical attire
Credit: Jacob Odama

thinking and cares only about themselves. They are self-centered, exploitative, and driven by power. This type of leader prioritises their own interests over those of the Collective. In contrast, authentic Transformational Leadership is a leadership concept focused on social responsibility and the common good.

Chapter 4
The HOW of Leadership –
the Leader as a Servant & Steward

"A leader takes people where they want to go.

A great leader takes people where they don't necessarily want to go, but ought to be."

Rosalynn Carter, Former First Lady of the US

(the wife of former US President, Jimmy Carter)

The Servant Leader takes people where they ought to go by providing guidance and support, rather than simply giving orders. This entails enabling individuals to assume Ownership, including for their personal and professional development. This is a place that people may not generally want to go, as personal and professional development can be difficult due to factors such as comfort zones, fear of failure, self-doubt, resistance to change and lack of support. For example, public speaking is one of the most common fears among people. It is estimated that up to 75% of people experience some level of anxiety or fear when speaking in public. Overcoming these challenges often requires intentional effort, persistence and a willingness to embrace discomfort and uncertainty.

Servant Leadership is a people-centric approach that concerns the physical, emotional, mental and spiritual well-being of both people and the leader. In 2008, Professor Sen Sendjaya of Monash University simplified the concept of Servant Leadership by condensing the original list of 35 behaviours into six key dimensions. The initial 35-item *Servant Leadership Behaviour Scale* was a commonly employed measure of a Servant Leader's behaviour, with both qualitative and quantitative studies conducted to establish its psychometric properties.

The six Servant Leadership dimensions measured are as follows:

Dimension 1: Authentic Self

Being your Authentic Self is a profound dedication to remain genuine and truthful, which entails recognising your True Self and living in accordance with your values. Attaining this authenticity requires continuous self-awareness, which involves being appropriately open about your emotions and beliefs.

My experience of this dimension from international banking

During my tenure in the corporate world between Milan and London, the second bank I was employed at mandated that all employees participate in their induction programme. Despite the importance of profitability, the bank placed significant emphasis on conducting business ethically and in accordance with their values. The bank's Organisational Development (OD) team oversaw the induction, with a focus on the company's culture. They encouraged a culture of honesty and transparency, urging employees to adopt an attitude of being *disarmingly honest*. This was expected not only in how we interacted amongst our colleagues, but also with our clients. This honourable approach was well received by industry as the financial world was still reeling from the *Global Financial Crisis* (GFC). Years of excessive risk-taking by global financial institutions, and the bursting of the US housing bubble, culminated in the perfect storm for a financial crisis. Consequently, the GFC is regarded as the most serious financial crisis since the *Great Depression* (1929- 1939).

To a lot of people, the articulate, educated, yet elusive banker exuded an aura of having knowledge beyond their grasp. As a result, people invested their money even though they did not understand several of the complex financial instruments. The perception was that the bankers knew what they were doing, however this changed after billions of US Dollars were lost. Notwithstanding the romantic aspect of the smooth talker, being disarmingly honest came across as authentic and helped to build trust.

Dimension 2: Covenantal Relationship (mutual agreement)

This dimension is founded on a mutual expectation between the people and the leader, marked by shared objectives, shared values, mutual trust, respect and ethical behaviour. Broadly speaking, people expect the leader to keep them safe, meet their needs and lead by example, whilst providing leadership towards a vision. Conversely, the leader expects people to contribute towards the mission. This mutual expectation serves as the foundation for the mutual agreement, which centres around three key mutual understandings.

1. Clarity of role

It is imperative for employees to have a clear understanding of their roles and responsibilities, along with how they align with the organisation's vision and objectives. Despite having a clear job description, there might be instances where an employee encounters a situation that falls outside the scope of their role, causing them to feel uncertain about what action to take.

Commander's Intent is a concept used in the US military to address such scenarios and is closely connected with Command and Control. Commander's Intent is the leader's description and definition of what a successful mission will look like when goals are met.

Photo credit: Jeremy Bezanger

Although planning begins with the Mission Statement, it is the Commander's Intent which describes the desired outcome. This concept can apply to multiple disciplines, important that there is an understanding and alignment with the leader's intention.

2. Commitment to the role

When employees commit to fulfilling their designated roles and responsibilities, it fosters a sense of Ownership. Having a culture of accountability avoids the need to micro-manage. Given that the leader bears ultimate responsibility for delivering results, it is prudent to establish checks and balances. Therefore, to ensure proper oversight, it is recommended for the leader to trust but verify.

Note: Having clarity on mutual expectations and a commitment to fulfil this expectation provides the framework within which people can operate freely.

Even with a clear understanding of one's role and a strong dedication to it, there may arise circumstances where the appropriate course of action is not readily apparent. In a Command and Control structure, the leader gives orders and expects compliance, be it in a centralised or a decentralised manner. A decentralised approach serves to empower people, enabling adaptive leadership appropriate to the situation. This is a form of distributed leadership, which author James P. Spillane describes as "primarily focused on leadership practices rather than individual leaders or their roles, functions, routines and structures." This does not mean the elimination of a formal leadership structure or the democratisation of the leadership process. This style of leadership necessitates a strong and central figure who is both capable and willing to develop people and promote the distribution of leadership responsibilities. This approach is generally effective when external variables impacting your organisation are known. For instance, in military settings, these variables include a recognised adversary, a well-defined location and known allies.

However, in the multi-polar post-Cold War environment it became increasingly apparent that these **variables were often unknown,** consequently it did not provide the necessary empowerment for people on the ground to take action in a VUCA environment. The idea of decentralised leadership was reviewed, and the Mission Command concept was introduced to complement it. Although it can be viewed as a type of decentralised command, it is based on three principles: Commander's Intent, mission-type orders and decentralised execution.

These principles are explained further below:

- The Commander's Intent: This is a flexible and adaptable approach that aligns with the organisation's vision. Effective communication is crucial to galvanise the vision and empower individuals to modify the plan when obstacles arise. This approach encourages Shared Ownership and is essential in chaotic environments where unknown variables are prevalent.

- Mission-type orders: This allows leaders to define the mission objectives while granting people the flexibility to use their own initiative, creativity, and decision-making skills to achieve it. This approach is particularly effective in complex and unpredictable situations and can improve organisational agility, problem-solving capabilities and innovation.

- Decentralised execution: This is a leadership approach in which decision-making authority and responsibility are distributed throughout an organisation, rather than being centralised at the top. In this approach, each team or individual is given the autonomy to make decisions and take actions that align with the organisation's overall goals and objectives.

From a business perspective, Mission Command means giving employees the autonomy to make decisions and take actions that align with the organisation's overall goals and objectives, similar to the concept of an Ownership-driven life. Leaders define the mission, providing resources and support to accomplish the mission, but employees are given the freedom to determine the approach. A comparison of Command and Control with Mission Command:

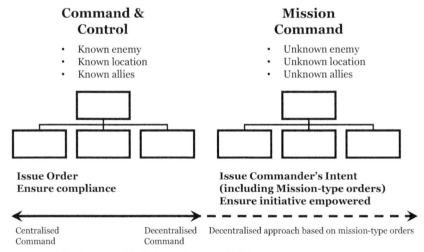

Source: Lt Col E. M. Lopez, US Air Force Reserve, C. Chiste 2022

Although Mission Command may be a fairly new doctrine, this is based on the timeless guiding principle of **trust**. Underpinning Mission Command is the trust in your people to plan, coordinate and execute decision-making in an agile, yet disciplined manner whilst operating in complex environments. This gives the leader confidence in the mission. Prussia learnt this lesson the hard way.

After suffering a humiliating defeat to France at the *Battle of Jena-Auerstedt* in 1806, Prussia, who were recognised for having one of the strongest militaries in Europe, realised that they had to revisit their doctrine. Three decades later, following a comprehensive examination of Prussian doctrine, it was determined that an update to their field service regulation was necessary. The crux of their discoveries was that the French were able to maintain a high operational tempo by quickly relaying Napoléon Bonaparte's intentions and reasoning, and by allowing junior officers to take initiative. This approach left the Prussians stunned and bewildered. Based on these findings, Prussia added to their field service regulation the following:

*"If an execution of an order was rendered impossible, an officer should seek to act in line with the **intention** behind it."*

With this shift in thinking, soldiers were expected to exercise independent yet disciplined thinking, with the belief that mistakes were preferable to hesitancy to enable decisive and bold actions. This was a major departure for an army built on strict obedience to orders with fixed Centralised Command. Leadership accepted that people may err when taking action in the face of an immediate threat. This emphasises the importance of leaders having faith in their team's prompt actions aligned with the task's purpose, even in ambiguous situations.

3.   Open feedback

Providing positive feedback can increase employee engagement significantly. According to research, employees who receive recognition are 40% more engaged than those who don't. On the other hand, employees should inform the leader if they are unable to fulfil their role to address any issues.

The leader-people relationship can be visualised as a network with different layers, formally represented as an organisational chart. Although the leader's inner circle of closest advisors may not necessarily be listed on the official organisational chart, they typically hold the highest position in the hierarchy. In politics, the formal hierarchy could be the National Executive Council (NEC) of a political party and in business this could be the Board or Exco. In reality, the leader could be heavily influenced by a stakeholder or donor. To assess the robustness of the leader's inner circle, important questions for the leader are:

- Does each person occupy a strategic position within the organisation?

- What level of influence do they hold and what value do they add?

- Do they contribute positively to the group dynamics?

- Can I trust that each member will support me through difficult times?

My experience of this dimension from international banking

When I joined my second bank in London, I went through the procedural process of signing my role description. This evidenced my legal commitment to the role. It was made aware that there was a budget allocated for training needs, as is the norm for many companies. However, the key differentiator was that there was an overriding corporate message that the organisation was flat and that everyone was encouraged to speak up and be heard. I knew what was expected of me, with support available. Freedom to operate within parameters, based on trust in my delivery, promoted self-sufficiency through training and culture. This encouraged ownership and innovation.

Dimension 3: Transforming Influence

A transformative influence involves the leader inspiring and empowering people to reach their potential, ultimately contributing to a positive and **healthy culture**. While task focus is still important, the emphasis is on people by building strong relationships and fostering a culture of trust, collaboration and Shared Ownership. Creating a compelling vision and **inspiring people to pursue it has a transformative effect**, as leaders are able to bring out the best in people as they strive towards achieving it.

When a leader articulates a clear and compelling vision for the organisation and communicates it effectively, it creates a shared understanding of what the organisation is striving to achieve. This shared understanding helps to align everyone's efforts towards a common goal, fostering a sense of purpose and direction.

Furthermore, when a leader identifies and communicates the **values** that support the vision, it sets the tone for the culture of the organisation. The values can serve as guiding principles that dictate how people should behave and make decisions. When everyone is on the same page in terms of what the organisation stands for and what it is working to achieve, it creates a sense of unity and shared commitment. In a **healthy culture** there is a shared sense of purpose, high level of trust and open communication. A shared vision and values help to create this type of culture. By creating a culture that prioritises continuous learning and development, leaders can encourage their employees to overcome their fear of making mistakes and empower them to reach their full potential by discovering and utilising their innate talents and abilities. Additionally, this type of culture allows leaders to provide support and opportunities for growth, helping people to achieve their personal and professional goals. Greenleaf argued that the Servant Leader brings about transformation in people in multiple aspects, be it emotionally, socially, intellectually and spiritually. In addition to inspiring a shared vision, the transformative influence of a leader also involves coaching and mentoring to empower others. This process enables the leader to influence followers and create positive change, both individually and collectively. The transformative power of a leader can extend beyond inspiring a shared vision and include leading by example. Leading by example with integrity, empathy and a strong sense of purpose, providing guidance and support to help others become the best version of themselves. In fact, this concept is not limited to those in official leadership positions. A humble non-leader can also exhibit transformative power by demonstrating exemplary behaviour, such as offering a friendly greeting each morning, setting a positive example for others to follow.

When there is trust, it becomes easier to influence. This is similar to the psychology behind **social media influencers**. The rationale behind this phenomenon is that having a larger number of social media followers translates to a higher perceived level of authority and social proof. People perceive those with more followers as more credible and influential, resulting in increased engagement and growth in their following. An influencers endorsement could trigger the assimilation of new information, resulting in changes in their follower's preferences and behaviour. While the authenticity and quality of the followers is debatable and whether this constitutes genuine leadership may also be questioned, it is important to consider this in the context of Transforming Influence. As an example, before acquiring Twitter, Elon Musk approximated that around 20% of the accounts on the platform were either fake or spam. Nonetheless, his substantial following highlights his capacity to wield a substantial influence in shaping opinions and attitudes. From an equally important bottom-up approach, a culture which engenders interpersonal trust is central to organisational effectiveness. Three actions that a leader can take to help build **trust** are presented below:

Action 1: Consulting when making decisions.

Providing a secure and nurturing atmosphere where team members feel at ease in sharing their thoughts and emotions is paramount for leaders. This involves actively listening to and addressing the concerns and fears of the Collective.

When acknowledged and supported, individuals are more likely to take calculated risks without fear of negative consequences, enabling leaders to delegate and empower in order to achieve objectives. However, during a crisis or uncertainty, the leader prioritises safety and suspends Voluntary Subordination in order to take bold and decisive action. The trust built during normal times supports the leader in this role, as the Collective trusts him to act in their best interest. What sets a true leader apart from a self-seeking opportunist is his selfless intention. While serving with the intention of personal gain in mind, such an opportunist may compromise his principles and fail to act in the best interest of those he serves. However, even for a leader with the most honorable intentions, serving selflessly is not without risks.

This contrasts with a democracy, where consensus prevails, regardless of whether the leader views the decision as right or wrong. By consulting, the leader communicates their actions are aimed towards the betterment of the people, not the leader's self-interest, ultimately leading to the development of trust.

Action 2: Effective communication of vision.

Victor Frankl, a Holocaust survivor, highlighted the significant role of meaning in our lives. Meaning offers a sense of purpose, providing guiding values to evaluate our actions in pursuit of our goals. Understanding what you give meaning to and why you give it meaning provides you with a sense of control when you encounter challenges. In challenging times, you may say to yourself, *"Why am I putting myself through this? It is too hard."*

Your level of perseverance in pursuit of your vision can be determined by the meaning you assign it. When the leader effectively communicates the vision, by conveying his **positive intent**, it inspires trust among the people. When people can clearly see and understand the leader's goals and intentions, they are more likely to buy into the vision and commit to achieving it. This commitment can result in a deeper sense of **trust** and **collaboration**.

Note: Action 1 and 2 constitute basic two-way communication.

Action 3: Establishing shared values.

A shared vision often results in shared values, which foster a sense of community and connectedness, creating a feeling of belonging.

It is interesting to note that the word 'belonging' can be used in another context in addition to sense of belonging. The word belong relates to ownership, in the possession sense. If something belongs to you, this means you own it. By feeling connected to a community there is a consequential feeling of ownership, and the associated caring for the improvement of the community.

My experience of this dimension from the military

Research shows that people can influence those around them positively or negatively. We have all heard the saying, "it takes one bad apple to spoil the barrel." Thankfully, the opposite also holds true. The best illustration of this is **Madiba Magic**, which refers to the charismatic and inspiring leadership style of Mandela. A case in point being the 1995 Rugby World Cup where the Springboks advanced to the final, facing the heavily favoured New Zealand All Blacks. When the Springboks won the match in extra time, Mandela walked onto the field wearing a Springbok jersey and cap, which was seen as a remarkable gesture of support for a team that had once been associated with oppression. That moment is often referred to as Madiba Magic, and it is seen as a turning point in South Africa's history. Mandela's support for the Springboks helped to break down racial barriers and promote reconciliation in a country that had been torn apart by apartheid. The event was later immortalised in the Hollywood movie Invictus which tells the story of Mandela's leadership and the Springboks' journey to victory in 1995. Mandela was widely respected for his ability to bring people from different backgrounds together, to promote reconciliation, and to inspire hope for a better future. The word magic is used to describe his ability to inspire and lead people in a positive direction.

Everyone has the ability to influence, not only those in leadership positions. Someone greeting you in a friendly manner could be just the thing to put a smile on your face and positively influence your mood. This is explained by the concept of emotional contagion, based on the notion that positive emotions, such as joy, gratitude and kindness are able to spread from person to person.

The idea that a single positive action can create a ripple effect is further supported by the following psychological theories and concepts:

- Positive reinforcement: When someone receives positive feedback or reinforcement for a behaviour, they are more likely to repeat it in the future.

- Social norms: Repeated positive actions become normalised as social norms, increasing the likelihood of others conforming in a particular context.

- Social learning theory: This theory proposes that individuals learn through observing and imitating others' behaviour. In my Navy experience, I witnessed the effects of this firsthand, as I was motivated to follow the lead of two colleagues whom I observed being rewarded for their behaviour.

Personal hygiene is very important in the Navy, given the close living quarters, particularly aboard a ship. Since many diseases and conditions can be prevented or controlled through appropriate personal hygiene, such habits are essential for the good health of the individual and for the protection of the entire crew. In the Navy[7] the term stick man was the term for the cleanest and neatest officer under training for that week. It was a weekly award with two or three men consistently receiving this award.

Although I had always thought of myself as a tidy person, during inspections the inspecting officer would somehow manage to find faults in my presentation. My perspective shifted after two routine stickmen had been moved to my area of the dormitory. I came to the realisation that what I considered to be my best was not the Navy's best. By being flanked on either side of my bunk by these two serial stickmen, Midshipmen Ndlovu and van der Poel, it became clear to me that my habits before inspection were not as effective as I had thought. This was specifically relating to my ironing and boot polishing. Their positive influence resulted in me receiving the coveted stickman award on numerous occasions. Once my awareness was raised, there was a self-imposed requirement to raise the bar and rise to the occasion.

Dimension 4: Voluntary Subordination

This is the willingness of a leader to relinquish rights and interests, prioritising the service of the people, instead of using authoritarian or autocratic methods to lead. When people think of Servant Leadership, this dimension tends to come to mind. Gandhi's actions of humility became the personification of Voluntary Subordination. A leader can encourage collaboration by demonstrating a willingness to prioritise the needs of the people or organisation over their own.

---

[7] The term Navy written with an uppercase "N" refers to the South African Navy.

This communicates to people that their ideas and contributions are valued and appreciated. When people feel that their ideas and opinions are heard and taken into consideration, they are more likely to be invested in the success of the group as a whole. Additionally, by empowering team members and delegating tasks, the leader can free up his own time and energy to focus on higher-level strategic thinking and decision-making.

Furthermore, the leader must also know when to follow. This does not mean following blindly but being responsive to people's needs. Although people have given the leader the responsibility of being in charge, it is crucial for the leader to acknowledge that team members also possess the ability to think critically and may contribute valuable insights and ideas.

My practical experience of this dimension from the military

Whilst serving in the Navy, I was sent to Brazil on a deployment. After the ship had berthed, there was a requirement for the ship's hull to be searched by the divers for any damage or underwater sabotage devices. This was not a task which the divers were eager to undertake, for two reasons. The first being that the water was sewage ridden with risk of contracting hepatitis A. The second being the sheer size of the ship. At almost 150 metres in length with an 8-metre draft, this was quite an undertaking for only two divers. The search is carried out facing up as you face the ship, which can be quite a mind-blowing experience.

This is particularly the case whilst in the region of the keel, as you realise the entire 12,500-ton ship is lying directly above you. Despite being an Officer with the primary responsibility of driving the ship, I was also a diver. To demonstrate Voluntary Subordination and a sense of duty, I felt duty-bound to assist the divers with their unenviable task and lighten the load. However, the Second-in-Command declined my motivation and told me I would be putting the ship at risk. He reasoned that if I were to injure myself or become infected, this could jeopardise my ability to keep watch on the bridge whilst we cross the Atlantic on the return leg. I stressed the fact that I had been vaccinated against hepatitis to reduce the risk of getting infected from the polluted waters. Ultimately, the Command approved of my motivation.

Dimension 5: Responsible Morality (ethics)

Leaders faced with tough decisions during economic hardship must strike a delicate balance between maintaining moral legitimacy and utilising ethical means. Ethics guides behaviour in professions, communities and societies through moral principles and values, while morality is a person's individual beliefs and values regarding right and wrong. Ethics can be seen as a form of universal moral principles and values that take a standardised approach over a group of people, rather than on an individual basis. Ethical principles and values are often developed and agreed upon by a particular profession, community, or society to guide behaviour in a consistent and responsible manner.

While individuals may have their own personal moral beliefs and values, ethical principles and values provide a common framework for behaviour that is applicable to everyone within a particular group or profession. An ethical dilemma may arise when the right decision conflicts with the interests of stakeholders and donors. For instance, in business, leaders may feel pressured to disregard safety protocols, regulations or ethical practices in order to boost profits. Balancing competing values and interests, while upholding ethical responsibilities, can be a challenging task for leaders. To navigate complex ethical dilemmas, leaders need to practice self-management and make decisions that align with their personal values and those of their organisation.

Such situations can often create a moral dilemma, making it crucial for leaders to adhere to the principle of "doing the right thing even when no one is watching." By practicing ethical leadership, leaders can inspire others to do the same, creating an environment of trust and integrity. A code of ethics can provide guidance and establish a shared understanding of expectations, which in turn can build trust and promote consistency. It can also help manage risk by setting clear guidelines for decision-making and behaviour, encourage accountability by outlining responsibilities and obligations, and ultimately promote a culture of ethical behaviour and integrity.

My experience of this dimension from international banking

Job roles come with well-defined duties and responsibilities; however, the specifics of permissibility can often be ambiguous. Nevertheless, individuals generally possess an innate sense of right and wrong. The London Stock Exchange (LSE) upholds integrity in financial markets with their motto "My word is my bond", while the Baltic Exchange professes 'Our word, our bond'. During my early years in banking, a scandal unfolded involving hidden charges and fees associated with products sold by UK banks, such as insurance or funds. This resulted in compensation claims, most notably for the mis-selling of payment protection insurance (PPI), resulting in the infamous PPI scandal that inflicted a staggering cost of GBP 37.3 billion upon banks. Shockingly, it was reported that one-third of PPI customers were duped into purchasing useless insurance. The inadequate review of legal fine print allowed unethical practices to persist in pursuit of profit.

Another example was the manipulation of LIBOR rates by major banks, revealing a systemic disregard for ethical conduct and eroding trust in financial institutions. The LIBOR scandal, which occurred in the early 2010s, exposed the manipulation of this benchmark interest rate used worldwide to determine borrowing costs for various financial products. This scandal, described as "one of the biggest financial scams in history", caused by collusion among banks, had far-reaching consequences for businesses, investors and consumers. As confidence in Libor as a reliable benchmark waned, financial institutions faced higher borrowing costs. Lenders demanded a premium to compensate for the manipulated rates, resulting in increased risk and uncertainty. For instance, a British multinational bank faced significant fallout and paid a fine of USD 453 million (GBP 290 million) in a settlement with regulatory authorities. These penalties highlighted the severity of the scandal and the urgent need for comprehensive reforms to restore trust and accountability in the banking industry. The incident undermined the financial system's integrity, prompting increased regulatory scrutiny and industry-wide changes.

The question remains in these two examples: Where was their sense of Responsible Morality?

The Zulu description of the ideal leadership presence is **Isithunzi**. In this context, the term shadow is used as a metaphor to describe a leader's impact, but it should not be confused with the Jungian concept of the Shadow. It refers to the measurable extent of a leader's impact, specifically **influence** and **presence**. Anything that diminishes isithunzi is considered negative. Similar to gravitas, it relates to a person's demeanor that conveys seriousness and importance, often associated with leaders who display authority, confidence and respect. However, the subjective nature of gravitas means that some may wrongly assign isithunzi to individuals who have acquired wealth and status through criminal and unethical means, such as drug lords.

The Leader's Presence:

This can be described as a long shadow cast by the leader.

Credit: Jaanus Jagomägi

Nonetheless, 'real' isithunzi can be described as having gravitas in the form of influence and presence, underpinned by the highest form dignity. This trait is exclusively found in leaders with high ethical standards, who can be trusted to do the right thing. These leaders display Responsible Morality, serving as role models who encourage others to follow their lead. They establish a behavioural standard for people to follow, by exemplifying ethical conduct and making principled judgments.

Dimension 6: Transcendental Spirituality (calling)

Maslow's transcendence refers to the very highest levels of human consciousness. This involves a leader's ability to connect with a higher purpose, fostering a sense of purpose, direction and amongst people, i.e. an Ownership-driven life. This approach can increase motivation, commitment and galvanise the vision. In terms of Maslow's principle, it could be said that this dimension concerns the leader facilitating the Collective to transcend up the hierarchy towards self-actualisation and beyond. In an increasingly diverse and globalised world, leaders are often operating across cultural boundaries and adapting to cultural differences is crucial. Leadership requires **empathy** in order to inspire, motivate and guide others towards success. Empathy allows leaders to transcend traditional boundaries and view different perspectives as a fellow human being, putting themselves in someone else's shoes and seeing things from their point of view. Empathy reflects a genuine concern for others and creates a culture of respect, trust and collaboration. Ultimately, it is about the leader **caring** for the people and relevant stakeholders.

My experience of this dimension from living in South Africa

This dimension concerns raising the consciousness of the Collective. The Americans often cite Martin Luther King Jr's "I have a dream" speech. A renowned speech delivered by Mandela during the Rivonia Trial has gained notoriety in South Africa. In this speech, he shared an inspirational message regarding the potential for all races to coexist harmoniously. The relevant segment of his speech is portrayed in the mural displayed in the image to follow.

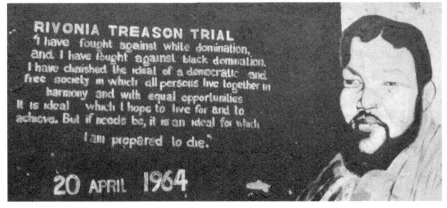

Credit: Francisco Anzola

Being the servant who provides stewardship

The philosophy of a Servant Leader places great emphasis on people's development, growth and well-being as essential factors for achieving sustainable profitability and long-term performance. In contrast to the one-dimensional leader often seen in the corporate world, who prioritises profit above any other value or goal. This approach to leadership was famously defined in Robert K. Greenleaf's 1970 book.

'Who is the servant-leader? The servant-leader is servant first. [...] It begins with the natural feeling that one wants to serve, to serve first. Then conscious choice brings one to aspire to lead.

He is sharply different from the person who is leader first, perhaps because of the need to assuage an unusual power drive or to acquire material possessions. For such it will be a later choice to serve—after leadership is established. The leader-first and the servant-first are two extreme types. Between them there are shadings and blends that are part of the infinite variety of human nature.

The difference manifests itself in the care taken by the servant-first to make sure that other people's highest priority needs are being served.

The best test, and difficult to administer, is: do those served grow as persons; do they, while being served, become healthier, wiser, freer, more autonomous, more likely themselves to become servants? And what is the effect on the least privileged in society; will he benefit, or, at least, will he not be further deprived?'

Both Servant Leadership and Steward Leadership are leadership styles that emphasise the importance of serving others and prioritising ethical practices. While Servant Leadership focuses on empowering individuals to serve others, Steward Leadership emphasises the leader's responsibility to manage and protect the organisation's resources and assets. This approach emphasises accountability and the importance of preserving resources for future generations. Although both approaches are valuable, Steward Leadership places a stronger focus on the responsible management of resources. According to Dr Kent R. Wilson's book *Steward Leadership in the Non-Profit Organization*:

All stewards are servants, but not all servants are stewards.

This means that while both leadership styles prioritise service to others, Steward Leadership goes beyond this to include the responsible management and protection of the organisation's resources, ensuring they are used in a sustainable and effective way. By understanding the unique aspects of each leadership style, organisations can develop effective leadership strategies that align with their mission and values.

Accountability for the stewardship of resources (Covenantal Relationship enhancement: Dimension 2)

To advance progress towards the long-term growth vision, the leader takes accountability for stewardship. This could involve directing, guiding, mentoring or coaching people, which reinforces the focus on caring for individuals within the framework of the Covenantal Relationship (Dimension 2).

My experience of this dimension from living in South Africa

As a result of widespread job losses during the *Great Lockdown in* South Africa, relief initiatives were launched to aid the vulnerable and those in need. Shockingly, special investigators announced that coronavirus funds were misused through corruption, fraud and overpriced protective gear supplied to government hospitals and departments. The June 2021 Auditor General report showed that some of the country's ZAR 500 billion (USD 30 billion) COVID-19 relief fund faced potential fraud, overpricing and improper beneficiary payments.

The report also revealed that contracts were given to companies with political connections or no experience, leading to overpricing and double payments. The report cited a lack of monitoring and oversight, which increased the risks of fraud and corruption. The Auditor General recommended taking action and implementing preventive measures. The report also highlighted the purchase of PPE at prices five times higher than advised. This money could have provided welcome relief to the needy, in a country where unemployment hit a record high of 35% during that period. This resulted in President Ramaphosa ordering a probe to gather information and assess the scope of the issue regarding government contracts awarded to politically connected individuals and companies.

Here are two accountability questions for leaders to reflect on to help them stay focused on their goals and responsibilities:

- Would you still be celebrated if the public knew what you did behind the scenes, no matter how important or renowned you are?

- Would you be dishonest for financial gain if there was no risk of getting caught?

The Steward Leadership dimensions can be thought of as existing along an Ownership Continuum as presented below.

Figure 21
Ownership Continuum:
Breakdown of the Steward Leadership dimensions

Centralised Approach		Decentralised Approach	
Total Ownership	Warrior Leadership	Steward Leadership	Shared Ownership
	To Survive (crisis)	Ownership Continuum	To Flourish (non-crisis)

Task-oriented with people in mind (to solve problems/issues)

People-oriented with task in mind (whilst empowering)

A – Authentic Self
R – Relationship built on mutual agreement
I – Influence trans-formatively towards vision
S – Servant who practices voluntary subordination
E – Ethics founded responsible morality
S – Selflessness through transcendental spirituality

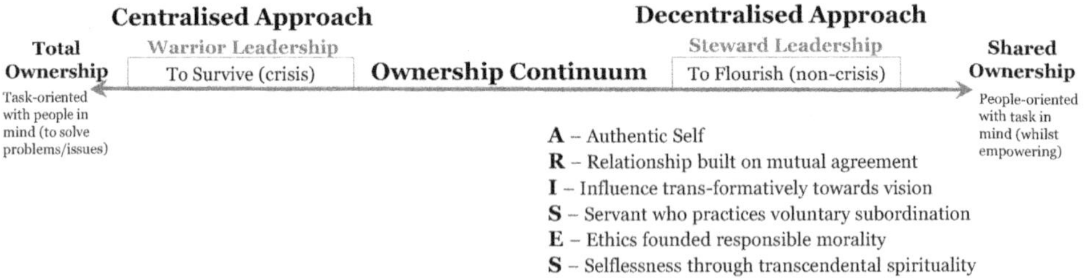

Source: © C. Chiste 2021

The above diagram shows dimensions represented by the acronym 'ARISES', which aims to empower individuals in the face of disruptive changes.

*"Rapid, constant, and **disruptive change is now the norm**, and what succeeded in the past is no longer a guide to what will succeed in the future.*

21st century managers simply don't (and can't) have all the right answers.

*To cope with this new reality, companies are moving **away from traditional command-and-control** practices and toward something very different.*

*The role of the manager, in short, is becoming that of a **Coach**."*

Harvard Business Review, 2015

In today's complex world, it is impossible for any leader to possess all the answers. When facing disruptive change, it's important for leaders to empower their people to adapt and innovate. Empowering people means giving them the autonomy, resources and support needed to make decisions and take actions that align with the organisation's goals. This approach can be effective in times of change as it allows for quick decision-making, rapid experimentation and the ability to pivot when necessary. When leaders empower their people, they create a culture of trust and accountability. Employees feel valued and supported and are more likely to take Ownership. This results in increased engagement, productivity and creativity, which are all essential for navigating disruptive change. Moreover, when employees are empowered, they can help leaders identify emerging opportunities and threats. This shared responsibility for change can reduce the burden on leaders and increase the likelihood of success, building a more resilient organisation that can adapt and thrive in the face of uncertainty.

While empowering people is generally beneficial, there may be situations where it is necessary for a leader to step in and take Total Ownership. This may happen when the situation is extremely urgent, or when the people involved do not have the necessary expertise or experience to handle the situation on their own. The next chapter introduces additional dimensions that build on Steward Leadership, creating the full range of dimensions of the Steward-Warrior Leader.

Chapter 5
The HOW of Leadership –
the Leader as a Warrior

"Hard times create strong men, strong men create good times,

good times create weak men, and weak men create hard times."

Author G. Michael Hopf

The fundamental idea is that history repeats itself in cycles. It serves as a stark reminder of how quickly our reality can transform. The world we know can undergo such profound changes that we may not even recognise it anymore, until it becomes completely foreign to us. The quote highlights civilization's potential collapse in catastrophic scenarios like nuclear wars, pandemics or environmental disasters

As our world faces persistent disruptions, some are better equipped than others to navigate the complexities of today's fast-changing environment. A case in point is the Great Lockdown of 2020, during which the public were instructed to stay at home to mitigate the spread of Covid-19. Politicians frequently emphasised that we were "all in this together" and that we were "all in the same boat". However, as pictures surfaced of Hollywood celebrities 'quarantined' in their luxurious mansions with expansive gardens, many families were forced to endure the lockdown in small apartments. Although we all confronted the same Covid-19 storm, it was clear that we were not navigating through the storm in the same boat. Those with greater resources were better equipped to endure the storm. This highlights the impact of resource access on an individual's ability to navigate through crises, exacerbated by the misappropriation of COVID-19 funds. In the context of Steward Leadership, effective management of resources is a crucial responsibility of leaders, who must ensure that people have access to essential resources to survive. During times of crisis, Steward Leaders prioritise the needs of the most vulnerable.

This approach aligns with Dr Kent Wilson's understanding of Steward Leadership, which emphasises taking responsibility for the well-being of others and entrusted resources. Additionally, the book provides resources to help leaders build resilience and navigate through crises successfully. Adopting a warrior-like mindset is necessary to tackle challenges and prepare for inevitable adversity, even during peaceful times. The Chinese proverb "it is better to be a warrior in a garden than a gardener in a war" underscores the importance of being prepared for challenges. This mindset aligns with Steward Leadership, which prioritises responsible resource management for the greater good. The concept of resource management in leadership applies not only to 'external' resources, such as assets and finances but also to 'internal' resources such as personal and professional growth. Moreover, effective resource management requires that leaders also manage their own internal resources. This means that leaders must focus on self-reflection and self-management to develop the necessary skills and qualities to manage resources effectively. Thus, in addition to acquiring external resources, leaders must also invest in their own personal and professional growth to ensure they have the necessary internal resources to meet the demands of uncertainty.

Building a home and maintaining a garden requires careful attention, patience and thoughtful planning, which are the responsibilities of a diligent steward. While a warrior can also tend to a garden, a gardener is unlikely to thrive in a battle without proper training. Therefore, in today's climate of uncertainty, it is crucial for leaders to acquire the internal resources required to upskill and meet the demands of the present. This means developing the necessary skills, knowledge, and resilience to navigate through challenges successfully. Just like a gardener must cultivate the soil and tend to the plants to ensure a bountiful harvest, leaders must invest in themselves to ensure they are equipped to lead effectively in times of crisis. By prioritising personal development, leaders can acquire the resources they need to tackle challenges with confidence and emerge stronger on the other side.

"Every time I read a management or self-help book, I find myself saying, 'That's fine, but that wasn't really the hard thing about the situation.'

The hard thing isn't setting a big, hairy, audacious goal (BHAG[8]). The hard thing is laying people off when you miss the big goal.

The hard thing isn't hiring great people. The hard thing is when those 'great people' develop a sense of entitlement and start demanding unreasonable things.

The hard thing isn't setting up an organizational chart. The hard thing is getting people to communicate within the organization that you just designed.

The hard thing isn't dreaming big. The hard thing is waking up in the middle of the night in a cold sweat when the dream turns into a nightmare."

Ben Horowitz

The primary leadership approach advocated is that of empowerment by inspiring Ownership-driven Leadership. However, there comes a time when the leader will need to do the 'hard thing'. This is precisely the reason for the additional dimensions, drawing on principles that have been proven effective in times of hardship. The military has a rich history of operating under adverse conditions, with wartime being the toughest of them all. Military leadership has influenced leadership in general by emphasising mission accomplishment, discipline, accountability, leading by example, teamwork and collaboration. These values have been incorporated into many leadership theories and practices and they continue to shape the way we think about leadership today. Additional dimensions are shared to help leaders become more effective in their specific discipline, rather than to glorify military leadership.

---

[8] A BHAG is a clear and compelling target for an organisation to strive for. This term was coined by Jim Collins and Jerry Porras in their book *Built to Last: Successful Habits of Visionary Companies.*

These additional dimensions are for when the leader finds himself in a dire situation requiring the adoption of a hands-on approach to ensure the safety and protection of his followers. It can be argued that the Total Ownership approach involves using either force or pressure to persuade the taking of action for the greater good. This may be necessitated when faced with the following two scenarios:

- **Scenario 1: Indirect approach using pressure to create urgency. The leader needs to implement a change management process.**
  The painful moment of the crisis has not yet arrived but is believed to be approaching. The leader needs to persuade people to change: We need to change to avoid or mitigate a threat.

- **Scenario 2: Direct approach involving bold action. The leader must act boldly to address an imminent threat.**
  The painful moment has arrived. This could be in the form of a crisis, possibly caused by a threat, chaos or a disruption, in which case there is unlikely to be enough time to implement a change management process. Bold action in the form of Courageous Selfless Action is required.

The use of coercive persuasion for the common good

Coercive persuasion refers to an active form of persuasion involving the use of force or pressure to persuade individuals or groups to take actions that are believed to be in the best interest of society or the greater good. However, there is often debate and controversy over whether the ends justify the means and whether the use of force can justify in the pursuit of the common good.

There is a passive form of persuasion that is equivalent in terms of serving the common good. This is referred to educational persuasion, which involves presenting information and arguments to inform and enlighten rather than coerce. This is used in public health campaigns and educational programmes to encourage positive behaviourial change through education.

In the case of scenario 1: If people do not acknowledge the necessity to change despite an impending threat, it could eventually result in a crisis. This poses a significant challenge for the leader, as people tend to resist change unless it is deemed absolutely essential. When there is a fundamental change in an organisation's underlying assumptions, beliefs and ways of doing things, this is referred to as a paradigm shift. This involves a shift in the organisation's overall perspective or worldview, typically requiring significant changes to processes, systems and culture. In essence, a paradigm shift involves a move away from the current way of doing things, towards a new way of approaching strategy, operations and decision-making. This shift may be triggered by a variety of factors, such as changes in the market, advancements in technology or evolving customer needs and preferences.

Despite implementing a change process to manage this shift, the process remains delicate, with the organisation exposed to significant risks, including:

- Disruption to operations: The significant changes required to the organisation's processes, systems and culture can cause disruptions to day-to-day operations.

- Financial risk: A change in operations often involves costly investment in new systems, processes or technology which may not yield returns.

- Employee morale and engagement: The uncertainty and disruption from a paradigm shift can have a negative impact on morale and engagement.

For an organisation to successfully navigate a paradigm shift, it is crucial to demonstrate a willingness to embrace change, challenge existing assumptions, question established beliefs, fully commit to change management by recognising the risks of not adapting and forming a cohesive vision of the desired end state. Ultimately, the goal of managing the change is for long-term success in a rapidly evolving world. As far as is practicable, change should occur as a natural part of the organisation's normal operations, rather than being perceived as a forced alteration. This is the challenge faced by implementers of change management.

McKinsey research indicates that **70% of change programmes** fail due to:

1. Resistance to change:

People's inclination towards routine and comfort is innate to human nature, making it difficult for the need to change to be recognised. An analogy can be drawn from the 19th-century frog experiment which posits that a frog immersed in boiling water will immediately attempt to jump out upon sensing the heat. However, if the frog is placed in tepid water which is then brought to a boil slowly, it will acclimatise and not perceive the danger. Continued raising of the temperature will eventually cook the frog to death.

2. Lack of trust:

Leaders are perceived as rarely putting the interests of the people first. Given the high rate of failure in change management, to facilitate the change, an adaptation of Kotter's model is presented below.

Figure 22
The change management model

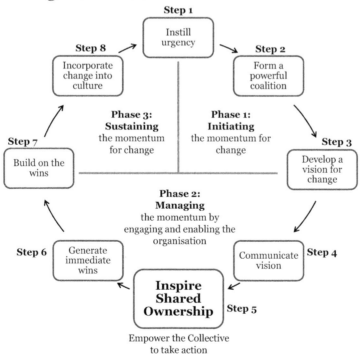

Source: Adaptation from Kotter, C. Chiste 2022

The eight-step model can be simplified into three phases for ease of application.

Phase 1: Creating the momentum for change

Creating a sense of urgency is necessary because it generates the necessary momentum to propel change forward. Excavations of extinct mammoths showed that some were still eating when they died, indicating that unexpected events can occur at any moment. A lack of urgency may result in the rapid emergence of an unfavourable future, leaving you ill-prepared for the consequences. Similar to the mammoths, you could find yourself caught off guard and unable to seize the moment. Identifying and forming a coalition with key change champions contributes to momentum as a force multiplier.

Much like the frog in tepid water analogy, there is a commonly held belief that significant changes cannot take place within an organisation until its problems reach a critical point and there are visible signs of an economic crisis. Kotter argues that this may hold true in cases where massive and complex transformations are required but is not the case for most change situations. To create a sense of urgency, even in companies that are achieving record profits, an effective technique is to inundate people with issues being faced, such as declining market share, potential threats in order to eliminate superficial optimism. Pressure in change management should be used carefully, considering people's well-being and capabilities. It should not turn into fearmongering but rather focus on empathy and intention. Developing a clear vision for change helps coordinate actions and align efforts.

Phase 2: Engaging and enabling the Collective

Having a clear and inspiring vision and using it to guide your path is crucial. In order to achieve this, the leader must inspire Shared Ownership to empower people to take purposeful action. To build credibility and confidence, the leader should start with easily achievable goals, known as low hanging fruit.

Communicating the achievement of short-term wins is crucial in lifting morale. Through consistent delivery of these easily attainable goals, the leader fosters trust. Research supports this, as the human brain subconsciously links familiar experiences that produce comparable outcomes, creating an association that becomes conscious when individuals recognise their emotions. The leader that follows through on commitments is regarded as consistent and reliable, i.e. the leader talks the talk and walks the walk.

Trust is built when a leader is perceived to have genuine, positive intentions that prioritise the well-being of the people. This trust is further strengthened when there is confidence that the leader will follow through and deliver upon his intention. This delivery concerns both the leader's reliability to follow through and his leadership ability to orientate along the Ownership Continuum from a hands-off to a hands-on approach (covered in the HOW of leadership). Even though there is an understanding of what builds trust, there is no guarantee as to when it will form. Trust follows kairos time, not chronos time, meaning that it is not a matter of clock time or specific deadlines, but rather a matter of the right moment or opportune time. Trust needs to be built through a series of consistent actions over time and it cannot be forced or manufactured. In other words, trust is a process that requires patience, persistence and authenticity. Trust cannot be achieved through shortcuts or quick fixes. It requires time to develop, as building a track record of performance, expertise, skill and reliability is a process. Empowering people to shape their desired reality by involving them in defining how accountability is enforced contributes to Ownership. By adopting this approach, a mentality of "shared purpose and shared destiny" is fostered, resulting in a united team regardless of the outcome. As a result, individuals feel supported by their teammates, resulting in the development of mutual trust. The term **'X factor'** represents an elusive, undefinable quality associated with success and influence. Likewise, the **Leader Factor Equation** was introduced in workshops and training sessions for teams and organisations, aiming to enhance leaders' understanding of trust.

The Leader Factor Equation

First order system | Link between systems

$$\text{The Leader Factor} = \frac{Intention + Deliverability\ of\ intent + Connectedness}{Leader's\ self\text{-}interest}$$

First order system

Intention: The perception of the leader's intention is influenced by the leader's integrity, transparency and communication. This should ideally be towards a vision of betterment, whilst empowering and ensuring safety.

Deliverability of intent: This concerns the two primary reasons for leadership failures, namely mistakes and psychological blockages. In the case of mistakes, this is the leader's understanding and ability to apply the HOW of leadership. Whereas psychological blockages concern the leader's dark (to be covered in Chapter 6). This impacts the perceived ability to deliver reliably. The ability to communicate effectively can influence people helping to amplify the credibility and relevance of the leader's intent, this can be through inspiration, information or persuasion.

Connectedness: This relates to the level of connection people feel with the leader based on shared values and genuine care for their concerns. A leader who is grounded in the reality of ordinary people, understands the everyday challenges. Decisions are based on a comprehensive understanding of the situation. Conversely, a leader who lives in a parallel universe is disconnected from both reality and the people. This helps to seal the enlarged container.

Leader's self-interest: This varies along a continuum based on the perception of the leader's selflessness or self-centeredness. This equation highlights the significant influence of the leader's self-interest on the other variables. If a leader demonstrates even a slight preference towards self-interest, it can be substantially challenging to regain the trust of the people. Recognising the influence of selflessness can be immensely powerful.

Leader's self-interest continuum

← →

Selflessness   Self-centredness

Phase 3: Implementing for sustainable change

To ensure that change is built upon and sustained, it is crucial to evaluate each outcome by identifying its strengths and areas for improvement. Additionally, reinforcing the change process is essential. The form of reinforcement may vary depending on the context, some effective methods include:

- Inspiring Ownership:
  Inspire a sense of Ownership by embedding the reasoning behind the change and making it clear that everyone has the power to achieve the desired outcome. People should associate the discomfort of the change process with the longer-term purpose of the change.

- Communicating that learning is a continuous process:
  Create psychological safety where mistakes are not penalised.

- Providing access to training and support:
  To facilitate the adoption of new systems and processes, employees could be offered training and ongoing support. Digital technology can automate reinforcement mechanisms, including digital training platforms and employee onboarding systems.

- Celebrating victories and giving recognition:
  Acknowledge successes, big or small, rewarding the change champions who helped make them happen. Rewards can be both intrinsic and extrinsic, providing a sense of significance and monetary incentive.

Given the high rate of change management failure, these measures are essential for sustaining change.

In the case of scenario 2: This occurs when the leader is faced with an impending crisis, requiring him to take decisive action, which may involve making tough decisions prioritising the welfare of the people.

When a crisis occurs, people are forced to adapt and change their behaviour. However, predicting the likelihood of future crises can be a challenging task that requires a comprehensive understanding of the situation. During normal business operations, it is common for people to become complacent and overlook the importance of preparing for a potential crisis, as they become too focused on the routine and comfortable familiarity of their daily work. While the adage, "it's not a matter of if, but when," may sound like an ominous warning, it should not be taken as a call to live in fear. This adage should be at the back of mind, where it is not actively being thought about, yet preventing complacency creep in. This serves as a powerful reminder to have contingency plans clearly in mind and to be prepared to respond to unexpected events. By staying vigilant and having contingency plans in place, there is a course of action to navigate the challenges that lie ahead.

The Crisis: The unwelcome guest that is bound to arrive

To discuss leadership in a crisis, let's first define it. A crisis is an urgent situation that requires prompt action to address the threat. Seeger et al define it as:

"A specific, unexpected, and non-routine event or series of events that create high levels of uncertainty and threat or perceived threat to an organization's high priority goals."

To enhance our understanding of a crisis and its practical implications, let's explore definitions from various experts and professionals.

An incident or situation that typically develops rapidly and creates a condition of such diplomatic, economic, or military importance that the President or Secretary of Defence considers a commitment of US military forces and resources to achieve national objectives. It may occur with little or no warning. It is fast-breaking and requires accelerated decision making. Sometimes a single crisis may spawn another crisis elsewhere.

(US Joint Chiefs of Staff, 2011)

A crisis is change – either sudden or evolving – that results in an urgent problem that must be addressed immediately. For a business, a crisis is anything with the potential to cause sudden and serious damage to its employees, reputation, or bottom line.

(Harvard Business Essentials, 2004)

Crises, catastrophes, and calamities are an unfortunate but inevitable fact of life. They have been with us since the beginning of time. It can be argued that they will be with us until the end of human history itself. In short, they are an integral part of the human condition. They are the human condition.

(Ian Mitroff, 2004)

A somewhat more positive perspective, in line with the term's original Greek meaning, is presented by Steven Fink, a crisis management expert. His definition emphasises not just the potential negative consequences, but also the possibility of a positive outcome. The term crisis derives from the words 'krisis' or 'krinein', which signifies a crucial moment where an important decision must be made, with outcomes that could be either positive or negative. Initially used in a medical context, the term was later adopted in psychology and psychiatry to indicate a significant turning point, before it became widely used to describe situations of critical danger.

A crisis is an unstable time or state of affairs in which a decisive change is impending–either one with the distinct possibility of a highly undesirable outcome or one with the distinct possibility of a highly desirable and extremely positive outcome. It is usually a 50-50 proposition, but you can improve the odds.

(Steven Fink, 1986)

These definitions share several commonalities, foremost among them being that a crisis can happen quickly and often without warning.

The diagram below offers an overview of the different stages involved in a crisis and their interdependencies, aiming to aid leaders in comprehending the importance of these stages within the wider context of organisational management. Ultimately serving to minimise the crisis impact and promptly restore normal operations.

Crisis management process: Interplay of actions pre, during & post

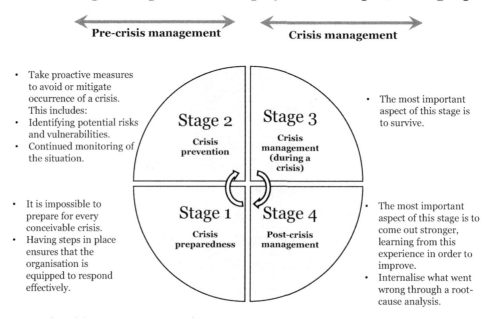

Source: Adapted from Tony Jacques, C. Chiste 2022

Stage 1: Being prepared for a crisis

To qualify as a crisis, an organisation must be facing a significant threat or danger. This forces the taking of steps to mitigate the possible negative consequences. Although the perceived potential crisis may not always materialise, it is crucial to note that many organisations lack a clear crisis definition. Identifying potential crises enables leaders to develop a plan and strategy. This could either be used or adapted in the moment, which in turn allows a faster reaction. However, even with a definition, the handling of a crisis is never seamless. A crisis is seldom viewed in the same way by everyone. Different priorities and values will cause people to have differing views. The perception of a crisis by only a minority could result in complications.

Stage 2: Crisis prevention or mitigation

The implementation of crisis planning and contingency plans can facilitate the introduction of measures to prevent or alleviate a crisis. After having consulted experts and his inner circle, the leader will have to make difficult decisions.

Business contingency plans needed even in the 'good' times

Note:

A crisis could unfold at any time, whether in times of prosperity (expansion) or downturn (contraction).

A crisis may manifest itself in different ways, be it intentional or unintentional.

Unintentional crisis	Intentional crisis
1. Natural disasters	1. Terrorism or sabotage
2. Disease outbreaks	2. Hostile takeovers
3. Economic downturn	3. Poor employee relationships
4. Political changes, conflict/war	4. Poor risk management
5. Technical glitches	5. Workplace violence (strikes)
6. Product failure	6. **Toxic Leadership**

Source: Ulmer, Sellnow and Seeger 2006, M. Brownrigg and C. Chiste 2022.

Toxic Leadership being listed as an 'intentional crisis' means it is avoidable. Understanding this is crucial to prevent unethical behaviour by leaders that is harmful and counterproductive. Weak organisational culture is often associated with Toxic Leadership, underscoring the critical need to address and prevent such unethical leadership behaviour. The US Army's 'Leadership Bible' (Army Doctrinal Publication 6-22) provides the following definition: *"The demonstration of leader behaviours that violate one or more of the Army's core leader competencies or Army Values, preventing a climate conducive to mission accomplishment."*

Stage 3: Managing the crisis

During a crisis, activating your crisis management plan is crucial. Additionally, there are other crucial steps to consider, such as:

- Prioritise safety: The safety and well-being of individuals should be the top priority. Leaders should take steps to ensure that people are safe and secure and that any immediate threats are addressed.

- Remain calm: It is important to remain calm and composed. Panic and chaos can exacerbate the situation and make it more difficult to manage. Leaders should hold the space to create a sense of stability and control.

- Establish clear roles: Establishing clear roles and responsibilities for all team members ensures effective collaboration in crisis management.

- Gather information: To manage a crisis, leaders must have accurate information about the situation, i.e. its cause, impact and potential risks.

- Adapt the plan of action: After stabilising the situation, leaders must create a flexible plan of action that considers the needs of all stakeholders.

- Provide ongoing communication: During a crisis, regular communication with all stakeholders is critical.

Stage 4: Post-crisis management

To emerge stronger and prevent future crises, it is essential to identify the root cause of a crisis and take corrective actions after the crisis has subsided. The Stoic philosopher, Epictetus, reminds us that "circumstances don't make the man, they only reveal him to himself." External circumstances test your character but do not have the final say in shaping who you are. Your reaction to adversity can either reveal your strengths and virtues or expose your weaknesses. When you internalise the lessons learned, you have a chance to draw power from adversity and improve your weaker areas. As the proverb says, "the strongest steel is forged in the hottest fire."

"The only thing necessary for the triumph of evil is for good men to do nothing."

Edmund Burke

Dimension 7: Ownership
(waive Voluntary Subordination for Total Ownership)

The primary function of this leadership model is for the leader to inspire Shared Ownership. However, when faced with extreme difficulties, such as a crisis, uncertainty or radical change, the leadership requirement shifts. In such cases. it is expected that the leader will take charge when the need arises, possibly assuming **Total Ownership**. The leader should not shy away from taking charge, despite any fear of failure, lack of support or potential backlash. Instead, it should be seen as an essential measure. As a leader, rising to the occasion is an expectation. This often entails adopting an assertive strategy that encourages bold and decisive action. Failing to do so weakens the leader's position, as the leadership vacuum will inevitably be filled by someone else.

It is important to emphasise that leaders must be held accountable for their use of power, ensuring that it is directed solely towards the benefit of the people and the greater good. There are times when the leader may even choose not to take action, either to consider other options or to position himself strategically. As Sun Tzu notes, *"Deliberately choosing to refrain from action is just as crucial as taking decisive action at the appropriate moment."*

Caveat: Beware of the self-proclaimed or titular leader. In exercising Total Ownership, the leader needs to understand the limits of authority. A famous example occurred in March 1981 after the assassination attempt on President Reagan. Secretary of State, Al Haig, declared 'I am in control' at a press conference. Critics viewed this as an inappropriate attempt to exceed his authority. Even the then US Vice President, George Bush Snr appeared to be confounded.

The term warrior may bring to mind images of ferocity and fear in the context of tribal societies. However, when it comes to the Warrior Leadership aspect of Total Ownership, it denotes the harnessing of warrior energy to triumph over adversity. Adverse scenarios can encompass a chaotic situation that escalates into a full-blown crisis (crisis management) or a subtler situation that is relatively stable yet requires adaptation (change management).

My practical experience of this dimension from the military

In the Navy there is the concept of the 'watch'. Whilst at sea, the watchkeeper is responsible for the safety of the ship, specifically in terms of collision and grounding. However, if it is felt that the safety of the ship is compromised, the captain has the right to relieve the watchkeeper of his watch at any time. On one occasion, as we were conducting manoeuvers at sea whilst in an elevated Combat State, there was a risk of the ship approaching the lighthouse dangerously close. The captain immediately stepped in and relieved the watchkeeper of his duty. The captain exercised Total Ownership to avoid a crisis. Below is a conceptual representation of how the orientation on the Ownership Continuum shifts to the left to ensure safety during times of crisis.

Figure 23
Ownership Continuum:
Steward Leadership impacted by a crisis causing a pivot

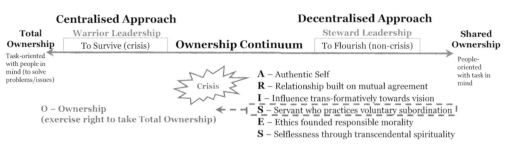

Source: © C. Chiste 2021

> **Note:** A crisis temporarily interrupts the leader's practice of Voluntary Subordination. The onset of a crisis can trigger panic and fear among people. To prevent any absence of Ownership, the leader takes charge by adopting Total Ownership. This moves the orientation on the continuum from the Steward Leader (on the right) towards the Warrior Leader (to the left).

No Ownership means no leadership

Energy is a dynamic and pervasive force that can transform between forms. Leaders must recognise that the people they lead, be it a team, organisation or nation, possess their own collective energy, which manifests in either constructive or destructive ways. Constructive energy is productive, driven by love and exhibited by nation-builders. On the other hand, destructive energy stems from hatred and negativity, fueled by those with manipulative and populist agendas. The Steward-Warrior Leader cannot risk leaving a void in leadership, which may be exploited by those whose self-serving objective is the fueling of destructive energy. To prevent this, Ownership must be adaptively balanced between the leader and the Collective based on the current circumstances.

Figure 24
Steward-Warrior Leadership Model:
Ownership balance to ensure no Ownership vacuum

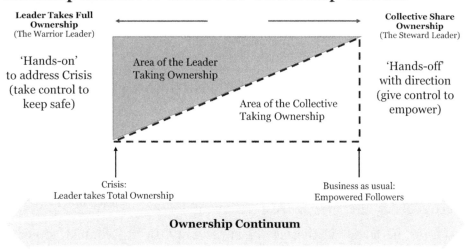

Source: © C. Chiste 2020

The area within the rectangle above shows that Ownership is always accounted for, whether this is by the leader (dark triangle area to the left) or shared by the Collective (white triangle area to the right), or a combination thereof.

In the absence of Ownership, the leader adopts a centralised approach stepping into the Warrior Leader, indicated by being positioned to the left side.

The cornerstone of this Ownership-driven Leadership approach is ensuring that there is no Ownership vacuum by establishing a solid leadership presence. The ultimate aim is to reinstate order and be positioned to the right side, where Shared Ownership can be achieved.

What is Warrior Leadership?

Warrior Leadership is characterised by the Warrior Ethos, which is essentially a mindset of commitment, underpinned by selfless motivation.

In South Africa, there is a historic rallying cry called **"Amandla"** (*Amandla Ngwethu*), an Nguni word which literally means "power". The cry was used to mean "power to the people", a call for the empowerment of the masses. This is an example of how warrior energy can be evoked, in this case it was to bring about an Ownership-driven life for the masses.

At first glance, Warrior Leadership may appear to resemble the Great Man Theory, bearing a resemblance to the actions of a hero combatting villains. However, a contrasting quality of the Warrior Leader relates to a softer, emotional aspect. This is the special trust and confidence placed on the leader in the face of uncertainty. In this context, strengthening teamwork and ethics is all the more important as it provides the sense that the leader/group has 'got my back'. This underpins the modern concept of a no-blame culture. The underlying driver is that of a guardian, particularly in times of crisis. This will likely require the leader to take a risk and make unpopular decisions, whilst at the same time attempting to be aligned with the sentiment and beliefs of the people. The support received by the leader will be a factor of the trust placed in him. It is important for the leader to recognise that the support given is based on the assumption that after overcoming the crisis or challenge, the leader will willingly return to Shared Ownership.

Collective empowerment: A fist raised aloft would typically accompany the "Amandla" rallying cry.

To clarify the Warrior Ethos, the Chief of Staff of the US Army authorised the following four principles to define this concept:

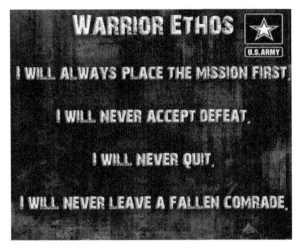

Source: US Army

These principles reveal the nature of the commitment required.

Principle 1: Place the mission first.

The order of priority is mission first, followed by the people and then the leader. This means that while the mission is the top priority, the leader must also prioritise the well-being and safety of his people. The leader must ensure they have resources, training and support for the mission while minimising personal risk. This aligns with the motto of the **Indian Military Academy,** which is engraved in their Central Hall named after Field Marshal Philip Chetwode, the former Commander-in-Chief of India. The motto states, "The safety, honour and welfare of your country always come first, every time. The honour, welfare, and comfort of the men under your command come next. Your own ease, comfort and safety come last, always and every time."

Principle 2: Never accept defeat.

The leader must adopt and display an 'unconquerable' attitude, even in the face of failure. The Latin term *morior Invictus* translates directly as "I die unvanquished", however, sometimes also translated as "death before defeat". In practice, even if you temporarily suffer a setback, seek ways to bounce back and continue persevering to achieve victory.

Principle 3: Never quit.

The leader should use problem-solving and creative thinking to tenaciously look for opportunities. Having mental toughness, faith in the mission and your people helps to further inculcate the 'never quit' principle.

→ A well-known saying which captures this 'never quit' principle is 'win or die trying'. However, should death occur, principle 2 would come into play as "if I were to die whilst trying, I would do so with an undefeated spirit... 'I die unvanquished'."

Principle 4: Never leave a fallen comrade behind.

The principle is firmly grounded in recognising the importance of team members for achieving mission success and ensuring their safety. This makes it both a moral obligation, as well as a practical necessity for achieving desired outcomes. Knowing that you will not be abandoned boosts morale and confidence, whilst fostering camaraderie, loyalty and trust. The principle of never leaving a fallen comrade behind is deeply ingrained in military culture and is considered a fundamental aspect of loyalty, honour and integrity. It means that a soldier should never abandon their fellow soldiers, even in the most difficult and dangerous situations. While the idea of literal self-sacrifice may appear radical within the framework of business, it aligns with the notion of promoting psychological safety. Research shows that once soldiers are convinced that they are being looked after, they feel that their own personal safety will be assured by others. This results in a feeling of being empowered to do their job. The practical implementation of this principle, whether in business or politics, would be subject to contextual differences. Nevertheless, the principle itself remains unchanged.

Even though the autocrat also assumes a hands-on approach, it is the selfless moral character which sets the Warrior Leader apart. This enables the leader to do the right thing, even though it may be unpopular. Consequently, the risk is that it could come at the expense of the leader's own career.

While the presence of the Warrior Ethos is commonly known in the US, it is present in militaries throughout the world. South Africa has embedded its Warrior Ethos within its Code of Conduct. **General (retd) Solly Shoke, former Chief of the SANDF** (2011-2021), emphasised the importance of this ethos when he said that although all members of the military are civil servants, they must also adhere to a Warrior Ethos of soldiership. This was reinforced by the subsequent **Chief of the SANDF, General R. Maphwanya,** when he highlighted that the military is the 'last line of defence' that the general public look to. The military is called the last defense as they are the final option to safeguard a nation's sovereignty, territory and citizens against external dangers.

CODE OF CONDUCT | FOR UNIFORMED MEMBERS OF THE SOUTH AFRICAN NATIONAL DEFENCE FORCE

- I pledge to serve and defend my country and its people in accordance with the Constitution and the law and with honour, dignity, courage and integrity.
- I serve in the SANDF with loyalty and pride, as a citizen and a volunteer.
- I respect the democratic political process and civil control of the SANDF.
- I will not advance or harm the interest of any political party or organisation.
- I accept personal responsibility for my actions.
- I will obey all lawful commands and respect all superiors.
- I will refuse to obey an obviously illegal order. **Warrior Ethos**
- I will carry out my mission with courage and assist my comrades-in-arms, even at the risk of my own life.
- I will treat all people fairly and respect their rights and dignity at all times, regardless of race, ethnicity, religion, gender, culture, language or sexual orientation.
- I will respect and support subordinates and treat them fairly.
- I will not abuse my authority, position or public funds for personal gain, political motive or any other reason.
- I will report criminal activity, corruption and misconduct to the appropriate authority.
- I will strive to improve the capabilities of the SANDF by maintaining discipline, safeguarding property, developing skills and knowledge, and performing my duties diligently and professionally.

Source: SANDF

The Warrior Ethos is essentially a set of principles that emphasises the values of honour, courage, selflessness and resilience. Resilience is an essential component required to endure and overcome adversity.

"In the 21st Century, change is the norm and **resilience** *is the new skill."*

Harvard Business Review

Amidst the rapid and dynamic changes in today's world, effective leaders should have the ability to strike a balance between a hands-off and a hands-on approach, guided by a selfless intent. Regardless of which approach the leader chooses, without resilience, how can a leader hold space for the collective?

Dimension 8: Resilience

Leaders who possess resilience can inspire people by modeling a growth mindset and demonstrating the ability to overcome obstacles. This is demonstrated by maintaining focus on achieving long-term goals even in the face of short-term setbacks, whilst remaining committed to the organisation's mission. Resilient leaders are better equipped to handle the stress and pressure of leadership roles, as they are more likely to remain level-headed in challenging situations, which enables effective decision-making. The first step to increase mental resilience is the mindfulness practice of going within to raise self-awareness. This is covered in detail in my subsequent book *Mental Toughness of a Warrior: Self-Leadership* (an overview can be found in the bonus section). The SPEAR model, developed whilst working with the military, provides a mental toughness tool to cultivate resilience in order to effectively carry out purposeful actions despite challenges.

My practical experience of this dimension from the military

According to the US Department of Veteran Affairs, military veterans, especially those who have served in active duty, are more prone to developing PTSD than civilians. Research suggests that the veteran suicide rate is an average of 22 suicides per day. The '22 Pushup Challenge' was created in 2016 as a viral social media campaign to raise awareness. In 2018, I developed training programs focused on enhancing mental toughness and resilience specifically for the Navy. Through Ownership, trust-building, emotional regulation techniques, attention management, reframing and connection, participants increased resilience. Resilience training in the workplace has been found to improve both personal resilience and overall wellbeing.

*"The **Western world has lost its civil courage**, both as a whole and separately, in each country, each government, each political party and of course in the United Nations.*

Such a decline in courage is particularly noticeable among the ruling groups and the intellectual elite, causing an impression of loss of courage by the entire society."

Nobel laureate, Alexander Solzhenitsyn

The decline in courage was cited by Solzhenitsyn in his speech at Harvard University as a cause for concern, as he questioned whether it marked the beginning of the end. He asserted that addressing the loss of courage is crucial for the West, as powerful weapons would be rendered ineffective without courage. Courage is an essential and fundamental virtue for a good and moral society. In addition to courage, Plato identified three other cardinal virtues: wisdom (prudence), justice (equity) and moderation (self-control, temperance). Although there are many virtues, these are the four cardinal virtues and are considered the most important. In fact, the word 'cardinal' comes from the Latin word for 'hinges', indicating that they are the pivotal virtues upon which others depend. Of all the virtues, courage is considered the most important, as it is the foundation that enables the other virtues. Solzhenitsyn's Harvard University speech illuminates the consequences related to the decline of the cardinal virtue of courage. Without the courage to act, none of the other virtues can be fully realised.

Dimension 9: Courageous Selfless Action

For many, courageous action involves a heroic act by a person who is faced with a fearful or uncertain situation. The perspective of courage as a momentary and isolated event aligns with the explanation provided by John McCain, a former US senator and Vietnam War prisoner.

"That rare moment of unity between conscience, fear, and action, when something deep within us strikes the flint of love, of honour, of duty, to make the spark that fires our resolve."

This definition of courage evokes images of the classical leader-hero who takes charge instinctively in a time of need, possibly risking his life. In business, this could be the dealmaker who does not buckle under pressure, who negotiates without blinking and backs himself to close the deal. To take advantage of this volatile, unpredictable world, the leader is required to make savvy decisions and move quickly. This volatility creates a moving target, with the original assumptions needing constant evaluation and adjustment.

Clausewitz recognises another kind of courage that goes beyond individual bravery, which is the courage to assume responsibility. This type of courage is essential for attaining strategic achievements. The leader will be called to make big decisions and should not fall victim to analysis paralyses. In the words of Shakespeare, the leader needs to *"be bloody, bold and resolute"*. For the Warrior Leader, the taking of bold action is underpinned by selflessness. It is more than doing the 'right' thing, at the 'right' time. There are times, particularly in a crisis, when the leader may need to make immediate decisions based on limited information. Not having the facts at hand means having to make assumptions. This is akin to driving in thick fog where you cannot see more than a metre ahead of you. Precautions are taken through actions such as reducing speed and turning on headlights and fog lights. Despite this risk, the driver continues the journey, driving with caution. This is a necessary risk in the name of progress, albeit slow, as opposed to stopping in the middle of the road and waiting for the fog to pass.

My experience of this dimension in the workplace

There are numerous heroic examples which come to mind, such as the South African Navy divers' daring rescue of the crew onboard the *Oceanos*, a cruise liner in distress. The sea on South Africa's east coast is known to be treacherous, perhaps Africa's version of the Bermuda Triangle. Abnormal waves of 8 metres in height are known to occur, these waves can completely immerse ships, putting strain on them for which they were not designed. Fittingly, the **Oceanos sea rescue is hailed as the greatest in the modern era.**

During this dramatic rescue, all 571 passengers and crew members were saved, due to the extraordinary heroic actions of Air Force personnel and Navy divers. It is worth noting that an act of heroism came from an unexpected source - the onboard entertainer, Robin Boltman. This individual displayed courage by remaining on the bridge until the end and maintaining communication with the rescue coordinators onshore, despite the fact that the captain was among the first to abandon the ship. Many of the aircrew and divers were given bravery

awards, with Navy diver Paul Whiley receiving the Honoris Crux Gold, of which only six were ever awarded in history. Even though the captain had abandoned the ship, the selfless efforts of those involved in the rescue operation ensured that hundreds of lives were saved.

The acts of the men on board the ill-fated SS Mendi during WW1 is another notable illustration of a courageous act. During the centenary in 2017 this tragic, yet inspiring event garnered significant attention, thereby raising public awareness. To mark the centenary, as the chairman of a South African military veteran association, I had the honour

Mendi Memorial:

With his fate sealed, a soldier is depicted with one hand raised to the heavens.

Credit: Christopher Szabo

to lead a diving effort to the SS Mendi wreck located at a 40-metre depth. Despite the harsh and icy waters, we paid tribute to these men at the site where the remains of the ship now lie at the bottom of the sea. The challenging dive conditions was a chilling reminder of the tragic event when the SS Mendi sunk in the early hours. However, this tragedy also became a renowned tale of courage that inspired and influenced the nation's spirit. As the ship carrying the South African Native Labour Corps men was about to sink, Reverend Isaac Wauchope Dyobha gathered them and motivated them to die like warriors with his now-famous words.

"Be quiet and calm, my countrymen, for what is taking place now is exactly what you came to do.

You are going to die, but that is what you came to do. Brothers, we are drilling the drill of death..."

After hearing these words from Rev Dyobha, the men of the South African Native Labour Corps then reportedly proceeded to pick up imaginary spears and shields and performed an African war dance, the dance of death. This would be their last action as their ship proceeded to sink to the bottom of the ocean. This remains **South Africa's deadliest maritime disaster** with 646 deaths, most of which were Black South Africans (607).

The action of these men inspired the highest medal for bravery to be named Order of Mendi. The badge of the order is oval to represent an African shield. Depicted on the badge is a ship, the SS Mendi. The national bird, the blue crane can be seen flying overhead. Behind the shield are a crossed assegai and knobkierrie (war club). The design is surrounded by a border decorated with lion pawprints.

Order of the Mendi

Note: Until 1992 the highest order for bravery was the Honoris Crux.

To make this relevant to everyday life, courage does not need to be to this extreme level, it is about being prepared to place the mission ahead of your own self-interest. Aristotle referred to courage as the first virtue, because without the courage to take action, none of the other virtues would be possible. Planning without action is futile. However, true courage comes from a place of **moral rectitude,** where people act on their beliefs despite potential harm. This **selfless courage**, often displayed when standing up for others, is not without risk, as negative energy can be redirected towards the courageous individual. The root of courage lies in the Latin word for heart is cor.

"Complex times require complete leaders...

*To be a leader in today's business environment, you need to use your **head**, demonstrate **heart** and **act with guts**."*

Dotlich, Cairo and Rhinesmith

In order to navigate through these complex times, it is important to not only prioritise the mind and heart, as commonly emphasised in mainstream literature, but also incorporate courageous action or 'guts'. Today's leader requires the ability to set strategy (head), empathise with others (heart) and take risks (guts) — all at the same time. It is also essential to comprehend which risks are worthwhile and to monitor their outcomes closely.

Drastic action during a crisis can have unintended consequences due to the complex and unpredictable nature of such situations. Hasty actions without careful planning may make things worse or create new problems, like strict lockdowns resulting in mental health decline, economic hardship and social unrest. To prevent such problems, it's important to assess the potential consequences of any action carefully and proceed cautiously, seeking input from experts and remaining flexible as the situation develops. Taking accountability can help prevent impulsive or overbearing conduct.

To become mindful of possible negative outcomes, a leader should adopt accountability and reject the idea that good intentions excuse any behaviour. Have you ever taken a bold step with good intentions, only to find that the result was not as favourable as you had anticipated?

Dimension 10: Accountability for the unintended consequences from Courageous Selfless Action

A common critique of the Servant Leadership approach is that if the leader places excessive emphasis on meeting the needs of the individuals, they may overlook the requirements of the organisation.

There are times when the leader may need to make unpopular decisions in order to address the needs of the organisation. This may come at a price, with the comfort and routine of the people negatively impacted. During a crisis, a leader may need to relinquish Voluntary Subordination and take courageous action, highlighting the significance of accountability.

The leader must reflect on the consequences of his decisions resulting from the hands-on approach of Total Ownership, which will likely involve applying some form of pressure or force. It's important to note that the implications of this role may not always be immediately recognisable, extending beyond the ordinary comprehension of unintended consequences. In **Systems Leadership**, one must comprehend all the elements that could potentially affect their organisation. This understanding enables the leader to carry out the HOW of leadership, providing context when applying the dimensions.

It is important to also consider that as action is taken to address a problem, another problem may emerge as an unforeseeable unintended consequence. It may not always be readily apparent how your action could impact the system beyond your organisation. The knock-on effects may be difficult to determine or prove. In chaos theory, this is referred to as the butterfly effect. When there is a sensitive dependence on initial conditions, a small change in one state of a deterministic, nonlinear system could result in large differences in a later state. A useful approach to facilitate decision-making is to have clarity of intention.

Clarity of intention facilitates determining the elements you need to consider, helping to arrange them into a hierarchy of impact. By ordering the hierarchy into bands, the challenge is often to determine their 'impact boundary'. Changing a part of a system may have the unintended consequence of impacting other parts of the broader system. To facilitate application, the leadership model presented in this book provides practical tools where principles can be easily understood.

Figure 25

Systems Thinking for Strategic Leadership

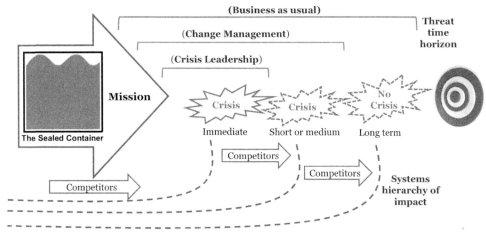

Source: © C. Chiste 2021

Note: In applying the analogy of the sealed container to represent an organisation, due consideration must be given to the outside forces and influences which could impact the system within the container. It is crucial to remember that the container analogy is not designed to isolate individuals from the external world. Instead, its primary objective is to ensure safety and foster social cohesion of the system within the container. Understanding **systems** and their interplay provides guidance on your strategy. Achieving long-term goals and objectives requires careful planning, decision-making and execution. Leaders are expected to analyse internal resources, comprehend the external environment and devise strategies that address challenges and capitalise on opportunities. Recognising and meeting the expectations and needs of different stakeholders is crucial when applying a systems thinking approach to **Strategic Leadership**. Having knowledge of the context is critical, asking yourself:

- What are the threats and opportunities?
- Who are our competitors?
- Can we form strategic partnerships with any competitors?

However, identifying an opportunity or deciding whether to take action can be challenging when experiencing stress. Stress encompasses any type of demand that affects the mind or body and can be triggered by various events or circumstances that can result in a fear-based emotion.

*"**Fear puts body and mind in crisis mode** and prepares us to run, fight or freeze. Everything not essential for survival shuts down so all our energy can be used to deal with what we perceive as an immediate threat.*

Crisis mode is like being chased by a bear. We don't stop and think about where we're going. We don't pay attention to what we might be stepping on or in. We don't pause to assess the best course of action. We just get the hell out of there.

We don't reach out or try to understand other people when we're in crisis mode."

Bob Van Oosterhout

Regardless of whether there is a disruption underway, or everything is proceeding normally, stressful situations are likely to arise. To effectively tackle any issues that may arise, it is essential for the leader to have the skill of remaining solution-focused at all times.

Changing leadership style in times of stress

Despite the possibility of incomplete information, it is often expected that the leader will make decisions in the best interest of the people. During times of stress, decision-making can be challenging when there is insufficient or unverified information available. While making decisions, a leader may need to contemplate his personal beliefs, values and intention for leading (their why for leading). Yet, there is a danger that the leader's actions in times of crisis may have adverse consequences, and as a result, ending his term in office.

The process of moving along the Ownership Continuum can be challenging for leaders. It requires ongoing self-reflection and a deep understanding of the context in order to evaluate any potential adverse effects.

Understanding the neuroscience of stress

Based on their function, hormones are sometimes labelled as either 'good' or 'bad' hormones.

'Happy' hormones, such as dopamine (pleasure), oxytocin (affection, trust), serotonin (learning, memory) and endorphins (reduce pain, enhance pleasure) are the so-called good hormones.

'Stress' hormones, including adrenalin (responsible fight or flight response to stress, enhances cognitive function such as memory and attention), norepinephrine (increases heart rate, blood pressure, and blood sugar levels, prepares body for fight or flight) and cortisol (helps to cope with stress), are the so-called bad hormones. Stressful situations could occur as part of our daily lives.

In times of stress, such as during a crisis, individuals tend to prioritise self-preservation and enter into survival mode. This can trigger the release of stress hormones and create an atmosphere of distrust. For example, during the Covid-19 pandemic, we witnessed news images of shoppers desperately filling their trollies with toilet rolls. This resulted in empty shelves with no stock for the next shopper.

In the business world, a stressful work environment can arise when companies undergo contraction and divestment of non-core businesses. Top-level decisions to implement cost-saving measures can trigger a knee-jerk defensive reaction that results in job cuts, as employees are viewed as a cost rather than an income-generating asset.

Moreover, a work culture that lacks a sense of Ownership can promote a blame culture of backstabbing where scapegoats are targeted. This can impede productivity and the quality of work, resulting in negative impacts on social structures within the workplace, resulting in strained relationships, diminished trust and increased stress levels. The leader plays a crucial role in moving the Collective from a low trust environment to that of high trust. This is covered in further detail in Chapter 7 (Safety along the continuum).

Figure 26
Impact of stress

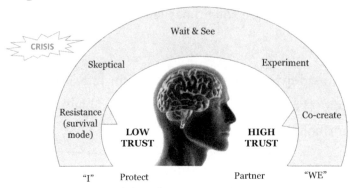

Source: Adapted from Judith E. Glaser 2014, C. Chiste 2022

As illustrated in the diagram above, people tend to prioritise self-preservation and shift into a survival mode in response to stressful situations. However, this is not the case for the Steward-Warrior Leader. This is because this leader has earned trust by consistently demonstrating care during regular day-to-day operations. The leader's empathy stems from a deep sense of connection, seeing the Collective is an extension of himself. This is exemplified by his prioritisation of 'Collective preservation' rather than 'self-preservation' in times of crisis. Moreover, this fosters a high-trust environment where people are motivated to emulate the leader's selfless behaviour, as trust is sustained.

Figure 27
Impact of stress on the selfless Steward-Warrior Leader

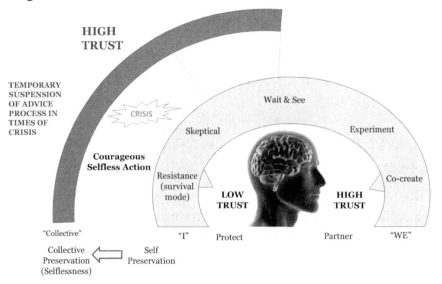

Source: Adapted from Judith E. Glaser 2014, C. Chiste 2022

The stress and happy hormones are linked to the two preceding graphs in the following manner:

Stress hormones (to the left)	Happy hormones (to the right)
Adrenaline (epinephrine) Norepinephrine (noradrenaline) Cortisol	Dopamine Oxytocin Serotonin Endorphin

Comparing the above hormones with the **Flow chemicals** below, we see that noradrenaline (stress hormone) is a Flow hormone. Consequently, the notion that stress hormones are simply bad does not hold, with these hormones playing a positive role in the attainment of the desired Flow state, which is an enabler in the achievement of peak state performance.

What is "Flow"?

A Flow state is widely recognised as the pinnacle of peak performance. Science shows that success and Flow go hand in hand. It is a term used by researchers to describe an optimal state of consciousness, those peak moments of total absorption where the Self vanishes, time flies and all aspects of performance excel. In the book *Stealing Fire*, four different aspects of Flow are identified:

- Selflessness
- Timelessness
- Effortlessness (merging of action and awareness)
- Richness (of mental and physical performance)

The enhancement of other aspects is greatly facilitated by possessing a sense of selflessness, especially when one believes in being part of a larger cause. Flow consists of the following hormones.

- Norepinephrine/noradrenaline (stress hormone)
- Dopamine (happy hormone)
- Endorphins (happy hormone)
- Anandamide (happy hormone)

Conventionally speaking, being in the 'I' space (the left-hand side of Figure 26) is generally not regarded as favourable, as this is the 'amygdala hijack'. This is where the individual is concerned with self-preservation, with the part of the brain responsible for rational thinking is 'hijacked', going into fight or flight mode. Although Flow stems from a combination of both stress and happy hormones, the key driver is selflessness. It follows that self-preservation is replaced with Collective preservation. Selflessness is an important ingredient for achieving a heightened Flow state. Furthermore, the belief that stress is inherently bad is a misconception, because **stress can be both beneficial and detrimental**, depending on the circumstances. Stress is a natural physiological response to challenging or threatening situations that prepares our bodies to cope with those situations.

Good stress, also known as eustress, arises from situations that challenge and motivate individuals to achieve their goals. It can provide a sense of excitement, stimulate creativity and enhance overall performance. Eustress can help individuals to reach their full potential and result in a more fulfilling life. Conversely, bad stress, also known as distress, results from unpleasant or harmful stimuli, such as trauma or financial difficulties. This can cause anxiety, depression and other health issues, hindering one's quality of life and impeding goal attainment. Prolonged exposure to distress can result in chronic stress.

The key is to recognise and manage the type of stress that we experience. By learning to distinguish between eustress and distress and adopting effective stress-management techniques, we can minimise the harmful effects of stress and use it as a positive force to achieve our goals and improve our well-being.

Hormones and leadership: Understanding the link

The impact of hormones on leadership is a multifaceted and dynamic topic that has garnered significant attention in recent years. Hormones, which are chemical messengers produced by the endocrine system, can significantly influence various cognitive, emotional, and behavioural factors that impact a leader's effectiveness. Hormones have been identified as significant factors in leadership, as revealed by research.

A notable example is the Whitehall study conducted on UK civil servants, which discovered that job-related stress has a greater negative impact on the health of employees in lower positions than those in senior positions. This indicates that while stress affects everyone, it tends to affect those lower down the organisational hierarchy more severely.

Research on primates provides evidence that high testosterone levels are associated with high status and dominance. This is particularly the case when the primate is under threat. Research on testosterone's effects on humans is less conclusive. Studies suggest that the interplay between testosterone and cortisol is a predictor of status and dominance in humans. Higher status and dominance are associated with high levels of testosterone and low levels of cortisol.

"In stressful situations, leaders dwell on the stressful relations with others and cannot focus their intellectual abilities on the job.

Thus, intelligence is more effective and used more often in stress-free situations."

Fred Fiedler, developer of the Fiedler Contingency Model

Through Emotion and Attention Management leaders can still effectively use their intellectual abilities in stressful situations in order to focus on problem-solving. However, the natural tendency in times of crisis is to be affected by emotion which often overrides rational thinking. This makes it difficult for leaders to engage in consultative consensus-based decision-making process.

Decision-making in times of stress

The leader's ability to make difficult decisions and effectively execute them during such times depends greatly on the trust built with their team. The Steward-Warrior Leader fosters this trust by consistently demonstrating care for their team members.

When leaders view the Collective as an extension of themselves, their focus shifts to preserving the Collective.

Making bold decisions in the face of uncertainty often requires the suspension of conventional consensus decision-making processes for the sake of effectiveness. The support for the leader to take Total Ownership is **conditional** upon the leader not continuing to exert such powers once the crisis is over and the leader acting solely in the interests of the Collective. According to Fiedler, a leader's expertise can only enhance performance if certain conditions are met:

1. Group compliance.

The group should willingly follow the leader. If the leader has credibility and has earned the trust of the people, the leader is more likely to be followed. The Steward Leader gains this trust in times of business as usual.

2. Effective communication.

Effective communication is crucial, as even minor misunderstandings can lead to significant consequences. The leader's ability to communicate the leadership dimensions positively and clearly is a key part of the foundational principles.

However, effective communication is a two-way process with the leader required to be effective in not only giving, but also receiving information. This is by listening to the people to understand their needs, concerns, sentiment and hopes. The leader can accomplish this by the leader's social interaction, intelligence gathering, feedback portals etc. In addition to communication, the other three **foundational principles** are identified as the leader having the ability to practice Self-Leadership (a form of Ownership), leadership intellect (often referred to as the grey matter) and an understanding of the safety needs of the people.

The critical requirement of Communication

Research indicates that people speak around 16,000 words per day, but as much as 90% of conversations are unproductive and do not attain their intended objectives. Advances in neuroscience have shown how the information we receive can impact our brains.

However, communication is not limited to verbal communication, nor non-verbal for that matter. It also encompasses neurochemical interactions that indicate whether we are inclined toward trust or distrust. A distrustful exchange could trigger fear, whereas a trustful exchange could result in the leader being more influential and impactful with trust being built. Trust is a dynamic aspect that can fluctuate during casual conversations, and a leader's capacity to create a positive impact determines a high trust environment. A high trust environment is associated with a healthy culture, which is the cornerstone of high performing teams. Through effective communication skills the leader is able to **influence,** this through:

- Inspiration (emotional): Inspiration is less about convincing someone of something and more about creating a vision. This vision appeals to emotions and shared values, serving to ignite enthusiasm and motivation for people to take action. For the Steward-Warrior Leader, it means to also inspire people to live an Ownership-driven life.

- Information (data exchange): Providing relevant information and engaging in dialogue (two-way information flow). In practice, this could be the We have seen how an environment of safety enables people to think expansivelyexchange of information in relation to a complete task.

- Persuasion: Ethically neutral and rational persuasion involves employing logical arguments and evidence to inspire individuals, eliciting a positive emotional response and encouraging action beyond formal jurisdiction. An influential leader is evaluated based on his adeptness in utilising persuasion to motivate people.
  Beware of the unethical version: Persuasion can turn into manipulation when it involves the use of deceptive or unethical tactics to influence someone's decision or behaviour.

In times of a crisis, communication could be regarded as a matter of life and death. However, a crisis often brings with it uncertainty and fear. An example being the *Global Financial Crisis* of 2007–08, the so-called GFC. This would go down in history as a phase of the *Great Recession* which lasted into the early 2010s.

According to the International Monetary Fund (IMF) this was the most severe economic and financial meltdown since the *Great Depression* of the 1930s. In times of crisis and severe job losses, people look to their leaders for institutional holding and guidance. They seek information on the assurance of their salary and safety nets in case of job loss. If the leader does not communicate this, the void will be filled by the agenda of others. This could include rumours, misinformation or fake news. In times of uncertainty, the leader's communication should be centred around three stages:

1. **Current situation** (where are we now?):

This could involve presenting the current reality, including the expected changes and their anticipated impact. Providing assurance that there is support.

2. **Desired situation** (where do we want to go?):

The leader's vision can range from crisis management to grand plans, with consideration for short, medium, and long-term outcomes.

3. **Action to be taken** (what direction should we take?):

The leader shares his expectations of what is expected from the Collective. This should not be conveyed in a clinical and robotic manner. This stage is broad, encompassing the ten leadership dimensions, i.e. the HOW of leadership for Total Ownership.

In a perfect world, the leader would be able to lay down the goals and micro-goals towards the desired situation. What do we need to do to get out of this mess and return back to normal?

However, this is not always possible, with the need for the leader to inspire the Collective towards an Ownership-driven life towards the goal.

My practical experience of this principle from the military

In times of crisis or change

The means and content of communication needs to correspond to the orientation on the Safety Continuum (Chapter 7).

As the Navy was going through a process of change, with the integration of former enemy freedom-fighters into the statutory forces. During this process many who had been part of the statutory forces felt that their future was in jeopardy in the 'new' South Africa.

The Chief of the Navy at the time, Vice-Admiral R. C. Simpson-Anderson, ensured that everyone was informed by releasing regular Navy Information Bulletins. This communicated the changes taking place, thus mitigating the spread of rumours.

My experience of this dimension from international banking

Times of business as usual

During my tenure in banking, the notion of having the freedom to operate was emphasized. On my first day in the office, it was evident that I would not be subjected to micromanagement as I was informed, "we don't do timecards."

I was given the freedom to leave the office at my own discretion and entrusted with the responsibility of promoting the business and securing new deals, as long as I remained within the designated 'tramlines'[9].

Creative solution-based thinking

Many leadership models tend to have one common denominator, that of the leader possessing leadership intellect. Nobody wants to follow a leader with zero intellect regardless of how eloquent, educated or connected he may be.

---

[9] An empowering term used in the corporate environment of Investec, meaning to operate within the framework.

Napoleon Hill refers to the ability to access sources of knowledge beyond the ordinary level of thought as 'Infinite Intelligence'. According to Hill, a genius is someone who can elevate the vibration of thought to a level where they can effectively communicate with knowledge sources not attainable through usual thinking. Hill regards it as the highest form of intuition, a force that gives order and origin to everything in the entire universe. However, the conventional focus of intuition is commonly referred to as sixth sense, which is the intuition that comes from paying attention to emotions. Having a better understanding of ourselves and others can greatly improve intuition.

Leadership intellect is a broad concept which in addition to intuition, includes creative thinking, logical reasoning, curiosity, problem-solving ability, mental agility, sound judgement, emotional intelligence and technical ability.

Can everyone develop cognitive abilities? Research on neuroplasticity suggests that the brain can create new connections and rewire its circuits. Leaders are expected to enhance their cognitive abilities, as demonstrated by former US President Harry Truman's statement:

"Not all readers are leaders, but all leaders are readers."

The human brain has a remarkable ability to reorganise itself by forming new neural connections throughout life, referred to as neuroplasticity. In recent years there have been advancements in less-invasive forms of brain-computer interfaces for clinical use, specifically the functional magnetic resonance imaging (fMRI) discovered in 1990. This imaging uses the blood-oxygen-level dependent (BOLD) contrast to measure brain activity by detecting changes associated with blood flow. Studies have shown that it is possible to self-regulate a region of the brain known as the amygdala (located deep within the cerebral hemispheres and believed to influence motivational behaviour), consequently changing one's emotional state.

We have seen how an environment of safety enables people to think expansively, facilitating creativity and innovation. However, for the leader, creative solution-based thinking needs to be accessed regardless of whether the leader is feeling creative or not. Even if the leader finds himself distracted, solutions still need to be found. Creating a thinking environment is an important consideration (covered in Chapter 7); however, having the ability to think laterally is another.

A useful technique to improve lateral thinking ability was put forward by Dr Edward de Bono in his book, **Six Thinking Hats**.

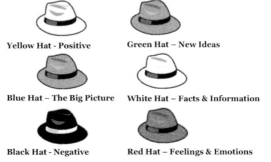

Yellow Hat - Positive

Green Hat – New Ideas

Blue Hat – The Big Picture

White Hat – Facts & Information

Black Hat - Negative

Red Hat – Feelings & Emotions

The rationale behind the success of this technique is as follows:

"Thinking is the ultimate resource. Yet we can never be satisfied with our most important skill. No matter how good we become, we should always want to be better.

Usually, the only people who are very satisfied with their thinking skill are those poor thinkers who believe that the purpose of thinking is to prove yourself right – to your own satisfaction. The main difficulty of thinking is confusion. We try to do too much at once. Emotions, information, logic, hope and creativity all crown in on us. It is like juggling with too many balls.

What I am putting forward in this book is a very simple concept that allows a thinker to do one thing at a time.

He or she becomes able to separate emotions from logic, creativity from information, and so on.

The concept is that of the six thinking hats. Putting on any of these hats defines a certain type of thinking. The six thinking hats allow us to conduct our thinking as a conductor might lead an orchestra.

We can call forth what we will. Similarly, in any meeting it is very useful to switch people out of their usual track in order to get them to think differently about the matter in hand."

De Bono cites several successful applications of this approach, including:

- The ABB (a major corporation in Finland) team discussions used to take 30 days for their multinational projects. Using the lateral thinking of the Six Hats method, the discussions were reduced to only two days.

- A researcher from a top IBM laboratory stated that this method had reduced meeting times to one quarter of what they used to be.

- Statoil in Norway had a problem with an oil rig that was costing about one hundred thousand dollars a day. After the introduction of this process, the problem was reportedly solved in 12 minutes, with the USD 100,000 per day expenditure reduced to nil.

- There are two similar cases: in one case the jury took more than three hours to reach a decision. In the second case, after one juror introduced the Six Hats, a decision was reached in 15 minutes.

- In an experiment with 300 senior civil servants, this method increased thinking productivity to 493%. Given that even if productivity increases by 5%, it could be regarded as a success.

The table to follow introduces an adaptation referred to as the **Six Roles**. This adaptation looks at the Six Hats through the lens of duality. Each role has an opposite method of approach, representing a different mode of thinking.

Duality of the Six Roles

Step 1: The Rational (Facts- driven)	**Task-focus (Role 1)** Consider facts for investment/divest-ment i.e. Why do we need to take action?	**People-focus (Role 2)** Relationship centred, emotion orientated, connector.	Step 2: The Collaborator (Emotion-driven)
Step 3: The Visionary (Vision)	**Non-linear thinking (Role 3)** Mind map, creativity, develop new ideas.	**Linear thinking (Role 6)** Processes, summarise outcome of thinking and determine path.	Step 5,7: The Guide (Road to vision)
Step 4: The Optimist (Best case scenario)	**Flourish mindset (Role 4)** Assurer of favourable outcome, explore the benefits and positives. Apply optimism when carrying out linear process thinking towards vision.	**Survival mindset (Role 5)** Assurer of safety measures to be taken to counter threats/dangers. Apply realistic unfavourable possibilities when carrying out linear process thinking towards vision.	Step 6: The Guardian (Worst case scenario)

Source: © C. Chiste 2021

Note: Step 1 is the call to action which kicks off the process. This is a facts-based rationale for the proposal, providing cold hard facts why the investment/divestment is needed. Step 2 provides a balanced view by considering the possible emotional reaction to any decisions. Step 7 re-looks at the process, after the consideration of possible negative eventualities of Step 5.

Figure 28

The Six Roles: Graphical Illustration of the role duality

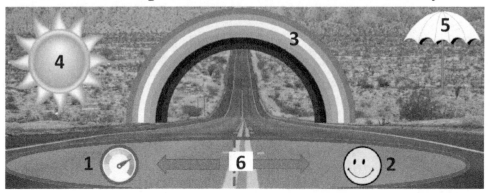

The above diagram has incorporated the duality of the Six Roles by utilising an analogy of a road trip through the desert towards a rainbow. This is done to simplify the understanding of these roles, which are contextualised as follows:

Role 1:

The gauge represents the facts. We are in the hot desert with no water and need to get to the rainbow to improve our livelihood. Along the road trip it could also represent the speed we are required to travel and amount fuel required for our journey (task-focus approach of the Rational).

Role 2:

The happy face being the emotional state of the people before and during the road trip (people-focus approach of the Collaborator).

Role 3:

The rainbow represents the desired outcome (Vision).

Role 4:

The sun represents the benefits of taking this road trip (the Optimist).

Role 5:

The umbrella being the contingencies in case anything goes wrong, such as a spare wheel in the boot in case of a puncture (the Guardian).

Role 6:

The road being the path towards it (the Guide).

How to apply the Six Roles process

The following has been adapted from a brainstorming scenario used by de Bono:

The scenario requiring lateral thinking: To determine whether to invest in new trains, engaging with the group can help identify potential issues and raise awareness by gathering relevant facts.

Step 1: Start with the facts and information (1 minute)

Present the facts. These could be around supply-demand statistics, demonstration of supply-demand mismatch to back up the need for new trains and economic factors driving the demand.

Step 2: Emotion (30 seconds)

Discuss your feelings and your experience in relation to what you feel about trains. Merely express your feelings.

Step 3: Vision/Creativity (1 minute)

To provoke further lateral thinking, assume the new trains are smaller, taking half the capacity they currently take, yet 20% faster. This is to stimulate the development of some new ideas from this suggestion.

Step 4: Optimist (1 minute)

Discuss any of the benefits or value of any idea you thought of. This is reframing the conversation using the idea of abundance and possibility. A useful technique is to start the sentence by asking "What if?".

Step 5: Guide – bullish approach (1 minute)

Summarise the outcome of the overall thinking of the realistic bullish view. Determine the steps and processes towards this view (this is Plan A).

Step 6: Guardian (1 minute)

Discuss the potential risks of your idea and suggest ways to mitigate them. Explore an alternative idea to address the issue.

Step 7: Guide – bearish approach (1 minute)

Summarise the outcome of the overall thinking by all the roles incorporating the risks presented by the Guardian. Determine the agreed upon path towards the vision should these risks materialise (Plan B or a modification to Plan A).

Note: All people involved in the deliberation play the same role for that iteration. Different roles help induce the hypothalamus to release different mood chemicals, rather maintaining one's negative default setting. Although de Bono cited some successful applications, it should not be viewed as a panacea for making simple decisions on all complex matters. Rather, it serves to promote lateral thinking and aid in the process of deliberation. The exposure to various roles can also have the effect of stimulating **curiosity,** what Professor George Loewenstein of Carnegie Mellon University refers to as 'priming the pump'. The reasoning is that curiosity requires some initial knowledge, as you are unlikely to be curious about something you know absolutely nothing about. Once you know even a little bit about something, curiosity is piqued. Research has shown that as more knowledge is acquired, curiosity increases. To start the process, Loewenstein suggests 'prime the pump' with intriguing, yet incomplete information. This stimulates curiosity to explore and discover. Leaders who are curious are proactive in their approach and better able to learn from their mistakes, being more open to feedback and more coachable.

Mental agility in decision-making

Another aspect of leadership intellect is mental agility. There may not always be sufficient time to apply the Six Roles technique, for which agility in thinking is critical. How can you increase your mental agility in making rapid decisions in confusing or chaotic situations?

The answer lies with a US fighter pilot named Colonel John 'Forty Second' Boyd, a veteran of the Korean War. He developed the **OODA Loop** technique, also known as an 'Agility Loop', to increase speed and agility.

Whilst serving as the Chief Instructor at the US Air Force Weapons School, he became famous for his standing challenge to trainees: From a position of disadvantage, he could defeat any of them in a dogfight within 40 seconds. His secret? He used the OODA Loop to great effect. This technique has since been adopted in business, politics and by many sports teams. It is a practical concept designed to function as the basis of rational thinking in chaotic situations which are high-stake. OODA stands for Observe, Orient, Decide and Act.

Observe	The first step is to collect the data. Determine where you are and what's happening around you. In order to make good decisions, you need to observe your environment.
Orient	The data collected needs to be processed to form a picture of the prevailing situation.
Decide	With the groundwork carried out in the previous two steps, it is time to select an action from possible options.
Action	Carry out the action, whilst being ready to return to the first step should another issue arise.

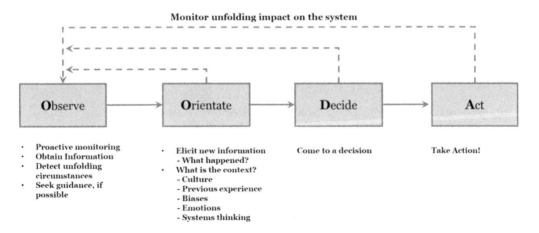

Information processing is about speed and agility. This technique also enables comfort with unpredictability and uncertainty.

Figure 29
Steward-Warrior Leadership Requirements Model:
The Leadership Requirements Wheel

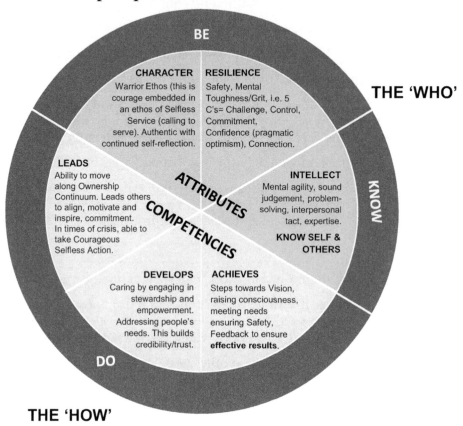

Source: Adapted from US Army, C. Chiste 2021

Note: The leadership dimensions can be broadly ordered in terms of three categories: character, competence and resilience, all anchored by the leader's commitment stemming from selflessness, i.e. caring.

This merges the leadership teachings of Dr Albert Wort from the University of Johannesburg with those of Major General (retired) John L. Gronski, who served as Brigade Commander in Ramadi, Iraq, commanding over 5,000 soldiers and marines during one of the bloodiest battles in recent warfare.

Character, competence, commitment and caring were identified as the key leadership elements by Wort. Whereas character, competence and resilience were identified by Gronski in his book, *Iron-Sharpened Leadership: Transforming Hard-Fought Lessons into Action.*

142

"The greatest danger in times of turbulence is not the turbulence – it is to act with yesterday's logic."

Peter Drucker

We see that the Ownership-driven Leadership approach of the Steward-Warrior model is a transformational approach to leadership. In the book, *Leadership*, Pulitzer Prize winner, James MacGregor Burns, breaks leadership down into two basic types:

- Transactional Leadership

- Transformational Leadership

The relationship of most leaders with their followers is transactional, where an exchange is made for services rendered. To explain the difference between these two forms of leadership MacGregor Burns refers to the works of Maslow.

Figure 30
Transactional vs Transformational Leadership:
From Maslow's hierarchy of needs approach

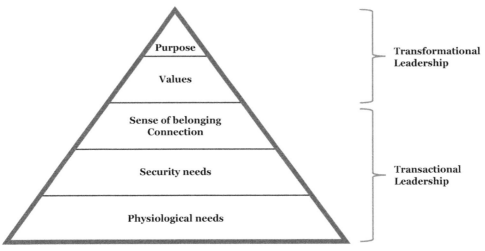

Credit: James MacGregor Burns, Maslow

Note: The meeting of the need relating to a sense of belonging can be seen as a consequence of the primary focus of Transactional Leadership, which is that of an exchange.

Transactional Leadership

Transactional Leaders are mainly in the business of addressing the "lower order" of Maslow's hierarchy of needs, primarily those related to physiological needs. According to MacGregor Burns, this form of leadership could also meet the psychological needs associated with a sense of belonging. These leaders essentially exchange rewards and privileges for desirable outcomes. This style is typically used by managers, with the focus tending to be on the basic management process of controlling, organising and short-term planning. This form of leadership is essentially one of exchange, either a carrot or a stick.

Bernard M. Bass put forward the concept of transactional factors, namely:

- Contingent Rewards.

    This is where the leader rewards people for performing.

- Management by Exception (active or passive).

    This is where the leader steps in only when something goes wrong. This could either be in the form of an active approach by tracking performance, or a passive approach by reacting to issues.

Transformational Leadership

Transformational Leaders engage the people on the higher order psychological needs, not only the lower order physiological needs. This is done by empowering people to reinforce feelings of competence, respect, self-worth and providing recognition that supports self-esteem.

These leaders also support and encourage people to be the best they can possibly become. It is evident that Steward-Warrior Leadership incorporates both Transformational and Transactional Leadership.

Figure 31

Bass and Avolio's Full Range Leadership Model

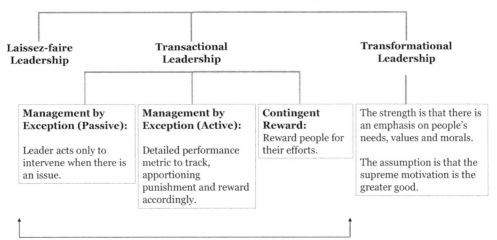

Most traditional leadership models fall in the Transactional Leadership category

Source: Bass

Bass regarded Transformational Leadership as the most effective form of leadership. To simplify this model, he introduced the concept of the "Four Factors of Transformational Leadership". This builds on the work of MacGregor Burns (1978) by explaining the psychological mechanisms that underpin transforming and transactional leadership. Bass introduced the term *transformational*, rather than Macgregor Burn's original *transforming*. Building further on the works of Kurt Lewin, who identified three styles of leadership: Autocratic, Democratic and Laissez-faire (1939) and Max Weber, who first described Transactional Leadership (1949).

If it can be said that Transactional Leadership results in the expected outcomes, then Transformational Leadership results in performance that exceeds what is expected.

The Four Factors of Transformational Leadership

(also referred to as the "Four I's" of Transformational Leadership)

Factor 1: Idealised Influence

Idealised influence is the emotional component sometimes referred to as charisma. It describes leaders who are strong role models for their followers.

Factor 2: Inspirational Motivation

Inspirational motivation can effectively inspire individuals to align with an organisation's vision and values, thus fostering a strong sense of team spirit. A powerful story behind the company logo, aligned with purpose and values, can inspire and motivate team members, resulting in a more engaged workforce. Utilising stories with symbols can create emotional appeals which build brand recognition and loyalty.

Factor 3: Intellectual Stimulation

This describes leaders who promote innovation and creativity by supporting critical thinking and problem-solving. They encourage new approaches and innovative solutions to improve the organisation.

Factor 4: Individualised Consideration

The leader's consideration of individuals encourages them to reach goals that are also aligned with the Collective. This factor concerns the leader's ability to provide a supportive climate in which he listens carefully to the needs of the people. Leaders act as coaches and advisers, trying to assist people to become self-actualised.

Below is a comparative table linking the "Four I's" of Transformational Leadership to Steward-Warrior Leadership.

The Four I's	Steward-Warrior Dimensions
Idealised Influence	Authentic Self, Responsible Morality (ethics), Transforming Influence (empowering).
Inspirational Motivation	Transforming Influence (inspiring vision)
Intellectual Stimulation	Transforming Influence (Ownership-driven life)
Individualised Consideration	Covenantal Relationship (open feedback)

Chapter 6
The Dark Side of Leadership

We all have defects. If you think you don't have any, can you really say that you know WHO you are?

The adage "don't judge a book by its cover" applies aptly to leadership. To illustrate this point, it is possible to have two leaders who both appear to be well-intentioned, but one of them may be deceptively good, concealing manipulative or malevolent behaviour behind the scenes, such as a psychopath or sociopath. Meanwhile, the second leader may genuinely have positive leadership intentions but may have unintentionally made mistakes due to yielding to temptation. Even those who strive for self-actualisation are not immune to succumbing to their darker impulses. Therefore, practicing Self-Leadership is a continual process to avoid falling into the Shadows of your own character.

We all have a Shadow, a part of us we hide, suppress or deny the existence of. This is not something to be ashamed of, with Carl Jung's words providing perspective:

*"How can I be substantial if I do not cast a shadow? I must have a **dark side** also if I am to be whole."*

Nobody is perfect, everyone has faults. An integral part of knowing **WHO** you are is also knowing your defects. If you don't own your defects, the risk is it will probably come out when you execute the **HOW** of Leadership. To operate in the light, and keep out of your Shadow, you need to ensure you are aligned with your personal core values and purpose. This requires self-reflection on a continual basis. Napoleon Hill makes the point that continued self-reflection is necessary regardless of successes stating:

"Those who succeed in any calling must prepare their minds to resist evil... you must examine yourself very carefully to determine whether you are susceptible to negative influences."

147

Literature contains a multitude of different archetypes. However, for practical purposes, it is useful to focus on the four core archetypes which essentially meet four fundamental human needs. These core archetypes can serve as a foundation, from which all others can be viewed as a subset. The table below segments archetypes by the fundamental needs they serve.

Core Archetype	Fundamental need served
The Ruler	To have structure and stability.
The Magician	To leave a mark (self-esteem)/problem-solving.
The Lover	To connect with other people/to care.
The Warrior	To take on challenges. To undertake a life journey. To live a life of purpose.

The Steward-Warrior Leader can be perceived as being represented by these four archetypes. Viewed through a Jungian lens, every archetype possesses a Shadow. Analysing these Shadows can offer a general high-level understanding of the dark side associated with the Steward-Warrior Leader.

Figure 32
The Steward-Warrior Leadership archetype map

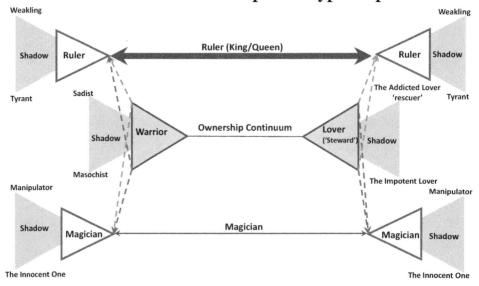

Source: Adaptation of Jung's archetypes. C. Chiste 2020

148

The Warrior archetype symbolises defense and safeguarding, but its Shadow aspect can manifest as extreme overprotection, leading to excessive domination and tyranny. Conversely, the energy of the Steward, which embodies the Lover archetype, is nurturing and considerate. However, an excessive amount of care may be viewed as submissive or weak.

The Steward-Warrior Leadership model centres on the interplay between these core archetypes. The dominance of only one would not yield the desired agility for leadership effectiveness in an ever-changing environment.

Although this model is centred on the Warrior and Lover (Steward) archetypes, it also possesses characteristics of the Magician and Ruler archetype. The latter being the archetype responsible for maintaining stability and order. Consequently, in the case of the imbalanced and immature Steward-Warrior Leader, there may be a hybrid of active and passive Shadows of these archetypes. Martin Luther King Jr understood this concept when he said:

Martin Luther King Jr:

Addressing a crowd from the steps of the Lincoln Memorial where he delivered the famous speech, 'I Have a Dream' on August 28, 1963.

"Power without love is reckless and abusive. Love without power is sentimental and anaemic."

In the context of Steward-Warrior Leadership, this quote could be read as:

"[Having only a Warrior archetype focus of] Power without love is reckless and abusive. [Conversely, having only the Lover archetype focus of] Love without power is sentimental and anaemic."

Niccolò Machiavelli, the renowned Italian philosopher of the 16th century, recognized the challenges that leaders face during times of adversity. He argued that to prevent revolt, a leader should be feared rather than loved. Although a leader ideally wants to be both feared and loved, it is challenging to achieve both.

Therefore, if a leader must choose one, it is much easier to be feared than loved. Machiavelli's insight highlights the delicate balance that leaders must maintain between respect and adoration, particularly in turbulent times. The downside is that fear creates mistrust and triggers survival mode thinking. When individuals are in an intimidating environment, they tend to focus on avoiding mistakes out of fear, making it unlikely for their true potential to be reached. The term **Machiavellian** was originally understood to mean the use of cunning and deceitful means to acquire and maintain political power, regardless of ethical consideration. However, the term has since evolved to encompass a broader meaning. Nowadays, the term is commonly used to describe individuals who are willing to manipulate and exploit others to achieve their goals, irrespective of the harm caused. Machiavelli's approach to leadership has drawn criticism for promoting an unscrupulous and ruthless attitude. Machiavelli's emphasis on maintaining power at all costs, regardless of the ethical or moral implications, has also been widely criticised for its harmful and counterproductive effects. His ideas have been associated with the rise of authoritarianism, particularly in the 20th century. Leaders such as Stalin, Hitler and Mao Zedong have been accused of following Machiavelli's advice in their leadership styles, leading to widespread human suffering and oppression. The Steward-Warrior Leadership model recognises a gap in the messaging that aspiring leaders receive regarding the HOW of effective leadership. This gap results in a lack of understanding that leadership involves serving others while pursuing goals. This model emphasises the significance of being able to move along the Ownership Continuum, where the ultimate motivator is a selfless intention. During times of crisis, it is essential that the fear experienced by individuals is not directed towards the leader, but rather towards the potential devastation that could unfold if the crisis remains unaddressed. However, the risk of unintended consequences always remains even for the leader with selfless intention as Shadow pitfalls always exist. This emphasises the need for leaders to continuously self-reflect to maintain self-actualisation when leading. To understand the Shadow better, let's explore its active and passive aspects in relation to the four core archetypes. The active Shadow is consciously hidden or suppressed, while the passive Shadow is unknown or unacknowledged. Both are important for self-awareness and integration.

Figure 33
The Four Core Archetypes and their Shadows

The Ruler

The active Shadow of the Ruler is the Tyrant. Possible root cause: lack of sense of calling, seeing people as a threat or objects to further himself.

The passive Shadow is the Weakling who embodies a sense of powerlessness and ineffectiveness. Possible root cause: lack of authoritative boundaries.

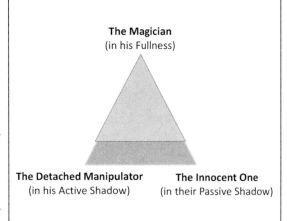

The Magician

The active Shadow of the Magician is the Manipulator, who uses the triggers of fear and guilt to motivate into action. A personality trait centered on cold and manipulative behaviour, often referred to as being Machiavellian. Possible root cause: need for validation, inflated sense of self-importance.

The passive Shadow is the Innocent One who pretends to be naive. Possible root cause: a lack of accountability or fear of uncertainty.

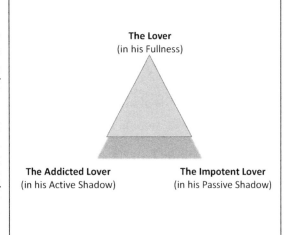

The Lover

The active Shadow of the Lover is the Addicted Lover, acting as the rescuer. Possible root cause: the need for validation or fear of abandonment.

The passive Shadow is the Impotent Lover who struggles to connect with people. Possible root cause: past trauma, excessive discipline causing a disconnect between the act of caring and the associated feeling, i.e. numbness of senses.

The Warrior	
The active Shadow of the Warrior is the Sadist, expressed as being emotionally detached or cruel. Possible root cause: workaholic. The passive Shadow is the Masochist, expressed by feeling like a martyr. Possible root cause: a lack of personal boundaries relating to lack of self-care.	

We all have a Shadow. The Chinese philosophical concept of yin and yang addresses the dual nature of all phenomena in the universe. It suggests that everything has an opposite: there is no day without night, no life without death. Every hard energy has an equal soft energy. Both energies are  strong, yet in different forms. Energy is always present, be it active or dormant. Leadership involves harnessing both active and latent energies. Active energy is outwardly expressed and visible, such as enthusiasm, motivation and passion. Latent energy, on the other hand, is hidden or dormant, but can be evoked when needed. For example, a team may not appear energised during a slow period, but with the right motivation and support, they can tap into their latent energy to achieve great results. Latent energy refers to energy that is present but not actively expressed or visible. It can be thought of as a potential source of energy that can be accessed and harnessed when needed.

The concepts of male energy and female energy relate to the idea that there are different types of energy that are traditionally associated with men and women. Male energy, which is represented by the Warrior Leader, is often associated with traits such as assertiveness, directness and competitiveness, while female energy, represented by the Steward Leader, is associated with traits such as empathy, compassion and collaboration. However, it is important to note that these are not inherent traits of men or women, but rather social and cultural constructs related to energy archetypes.

In the context of leadership, effective leaders understand how to access and utilise both active and latent energies to achieve their goals. This means being able to tap into the enthusiasm, motivation and passion of their team members, while also recognising and evoking their hidden potential when necessary.

Female energy can also relate to the empowerment of people through professional and personal development. Effective leaders who embody feminine energy of the Steward Leader, often prioritise the growth and development of their team members, creating an environment where individuals feel supported, valued and empowered to achieve their full potential.

The Steward Leader is unable to steward and empower the Collective if the Warrior Leader has not ensured the safety to do so. Duality is ever present.

The duality of power: Soft vs Hard

At the Military Academy, we learned about soft and hard power in international relations and politics. Soft power is generally understood to be the ability to **co-opt**, whereas hard power is the ability to **coerce** the other party towards your desired goal. In circumstances where the threat is not imminent, a collaborative change management approach is favoured.

However, the yin and yang are more than the integration of these polar energies, they represent the natural order of balance. Maintaining the balance of nature is crucial for sustaining a stable equilibrium. This balance involves both light and dark elements, as one cannot exist without the other. Every individual has a hidden dark side, known as the Shadow. This could be our inner urges, compulsions and dysfunctions that can drive us away from success and undermine accomplishments. Aristotle was clear that too much of any virtue is just as bad as lack of virtue. The right balance needs to be found. For example, excessive courage could be reckless and could get you killed. However, a lack of courage can make you cowardly. If you display excessive humility, you could be seen as shy and withdrawn. On the other hand, if you display too little modesty, you may come across as boastful and arrogant. The leader who ignores his dark side risks major failures, while one who confronts it achieves long-term success.

Exploring the causes of Leadership Failure: Insights on the impact of systemic issues and psychological factors

You may ask yourself, "how could a seemingly 'good' leader with the best intentions succumb to corruption?" or, "why does a leader go back on his word?"

When delving into the causes of leadership failure, it becomes crucial to explore not only the leader's application of effective leadership techniques but also the complex interplay of external and internal influences. External influences encompass issues within the **broader system**, while internal influences pertain to the leader's personal psychological makeup. Irrespective of the leader's genuine intentions to employ effective leadership practices, failure can still occur. An illustrative example of systemic failure can be found in the United States, where former President Donald Trump often used terms like 'swamp' and 'deep state' to refer to entrenched political and bureaucratic elites. Trump contended that this group operated within a larger system that hindered his administration's agenda and the interests of the American people. He believed that comprehensive reforms were necessary to uphold government integrity and accountability. Another instance is the prevalent practice of paying "facilitation fees" in parts of Africa. Although these payments may appear legitimate, they serve as a form of corruption, perpetuating a wider system of unethical conduct. By expediting services or transactions, these fees aim to influence decision-making and bypass bureaucratic procedures, thereby eroding the integrity of governmental institutions and diminishing public trust in the system. In both these examples, broader systemic issues can render an honest and well-intentioned leader, who strives to adhere to the rule book, ineffectual, akin to a 'lame duck'.

Furthermore, leadership failure can also stem from internal influences, originating within the leader himself. This failure is often attributed to traits such as arrogance, selfishness, aloofness or even corruption. However, these symptoms can be better understood as a consequence of the leader's inability to self-actualise and integrate his **Shadow**—the hidden and unacknowledged aspects of their personality that may influence their behaviour and decision-making.

By thoroughly examining the external and internal factors contributing to leadership failure, we can gain deeper insights into the complexities of leadership and work towards developing strategies to prevent and address such failures in the future. Although we see signs of hope and well-being around the world, there is also terror and corruption. This phenomenon of opposing forces coexist together. Therefore, the leader must embody the highs and lows, adjusting accordingly on the Ownership Continuum. This helps the leader to avoid operating on the Shadow extremes of the core archetypes. Nonetheless, the leader must be aware of the consequences of either extremity. The Warrior Leader can be seen to be combination of the Warrior and the Ruler archetype, in his active Shadow could be a sadistic tyrant. Whereas in his passive Shadow, could be a masochistic tyrant who is a self-destructive or self-defeating leader. Similarly, in the case of the Steward Leader which can be seen as a combination of Lover (Steward) and Ruler archetype, in his active Shadow can be seen as a rescuer who does not allow people to grow. Whereas his passive Shadow can be seen as a weak leader who struggles to connect with people.

Research shows that leadership failure does not come solely from mistakes whilst applying the HOW of leadership. Dr Olivier Guillet attributes two primary reasons for leadership failures, namely mistakes and psychological blockages. However, **psychological blockages** have been found to be a bigger contributor. Blockages are structural psychological limitations, manifesting as the Shadow, which often hinder leadership application and learning.

Reasons for leadership failures

Leadership Failures		
What is the primary reason?	**Shadow** (reason 1)	**Mistakes** (reason 2)
What is this due to?	Psychological Limitations	Contextual - based on the circumstances
What is the consequence?	Prevents the leadership learning process	Part of the leadership learning process
What leadership actions to address?	Improvement through Shadow work	Improvement through conscious awareness

In order for the leader to address the Shadow, continued self-reflection and self-actualisation is required. However, in the case of an actual mistake, this requires rational thinking and a conscious effort to correct it.

No one can become conscious of the Shadow without considerable moral effort. To become conscious requires one to recognise the dark aspects of one's personality. This act is an essential condition for any kind of self-knowledge. It is therefore usually met with considerable resistance. Closer examination of one's dark characteristics reveals that they have an emotional nature and a kind of autonomy. They therefore can have obsessive and possessive qualities. When an individual's Shadow takes over, their emotions may not feel like a deliberate activity of their own, but rather something that happens to them. The influence of negative emotions on individuals tends to be more pronounced in areas where their ability to adapt is already limited. Negative emotions such as sadness, anxiety, anger or fear have a profound impact on various aspects of our lives, including our thoughts, behaviors and overall well-being. They can shape our perceptions, decision-making processes and our capacity to effectively manage stress. It is important to recognise that when negative emotions arise, they tend to have a stronger impact on areas where we already struggle to adapt. Adaptation refers to the process of reconciling one's external world with their unique psychological characteristics. Through adaptation, individuals can develop the necessary coping mechanisms to navigate difficult emotions and situations. When this adaptation is the weakest, with its uncontrolled or scarcely controlled emotions, this could cause you to behave in an anti-social manner. These Shadows may manifest as psychological blockages.

The six major psychological causes for leadership failures

Dr Ronald J. Burke from York University identified six major psychological causes for leadership failures. These being betrayal, insensitivity, aloofness, perfectionism, selfishness and arrogance. Previously, we examined Shadow of the four core archetypes to gain a high-level understanding of common psychological blockages. Now, we will expand on these six specific psychological causes to make them more relevant to prevalent issues.

To consider these in terms of human needs not being met, these are:

1.   Betrayal/corruption (root cause linked to unactualised physical needs)

The leader who violates trust prioritises the drive for security over ethics, rationalising his actions as necessary for his family's financial security.

2.   Insensitivity (root cause linked to unactualised emotional needs)

Insensitivity could be in the form of being emotionally detached, which can stem from the fear of being emotionally hurt.

3.   Aloofness (root cause linked to unactualised emotional needs)

The state of aloofness may arise from a sense of detachment caused by the fear of rejection, resulting in emotional coldness. The leader who projects coldness struggles to motivate people and involuntarily creates dissonance among the people. The leader's lack of a sense of belonging may cause him to put on a façade of inclusivity, concealing his isolation and vulnerability. This could result in a superficial display of affection and concern, masking his true emotions. However, the vitality from human connection is absent. This dysfunction can become the norm, resulting in a social sickness that masks the True Self.

4.   Perfectionism (root cause linked to unactualised mental needs)

Some common underlying factors that may contribute to perfectionism include high personal standards, fear of failure or criticism, a need for control, low self-esteem and a desire for approval or validation from others. Additionally, childhood experiences, such as being praised only for accomplishments rather than effort or growing up in a highly competitive environment, can also contribute to the development of perfectionism. Failing to achieve perfection could be deemed unacceptable, resulting in a negative impact on self-worth. In an attempt to make up for falling short of perfection, the leader might accumulate material possessions, hoping to demonstrate success. Fear may motivate him to pursue a one-dimensional version of success, which could result in neglecting other important aspects of life, such as family, health or opportunities for personal growth.

5.   Selfishness (root cause linked to unactualised mental needs)

Selfish leaders are excessively self-focused, prioritising personal gain, pleasure, or well-being over others. In the context of business, selfishness is characterised by a display of self-centered greed.

Prof Andrew Lo from MIT compares a selfish leader to a spoilt child throwing tantrums to satisfy personal interests:

"This is when the natural human impulse to collect and consume useful resources like food, material wealth or fame overwhelms the constraints that maintained the social ties within a group.

This is akin to the child who does not want to be deprived of the latest toy, sensing that by throwing a tantrum in public the child's mother is likely to yield to silence the child."

6.   Arrogance (root cause linked to unactualised mental needs)

Arrogance is characterised by observable cases of leadership behaviour involving abnormal love of oneself, an exaggerated sense of superiority and/or a strong preoccupation with success and power. Behaviour such as this tends to compensate for a deeply sensed insecurity and fragile self-esteem. In its simplest terms, humility can be viewed as the antithesis of arrogance. For humility to be relevant, the leader must first have competence and confidence.

If the leader is not able to perform as a leader, humility would not apply. A leader with humility is a willing learner, maintaining self-awareness, seeking input and feedback from others. Understanding humility involves recognising one's strengths and weaknesses and applying it to leadership. Humility is an important but often under-discussed value of leadership, which can motivate people to be more open as the leader appears more approachable. If there is too little humility, this is expressed as arrogance. Conversely, excess humility could be problematic as it can be interpreted as being meek, obedient or timid. When introducing the humility concept, an appreciation of its complexity should be understood. It is necessary to clarify what psychological structures of humility we are interested in. The diagram to follow shows how main leadership failures result from psychological blockages, which can be removed by individuation. Individuation refers to the process through which a person achieves a sense of individuality separate from the identities of others and begins to consciously exist as a human in the world. Through the process of going within, it is possible to integrate the Shadow into the conscious personality.

Figure 34
Leadership failures due to psychological blockages

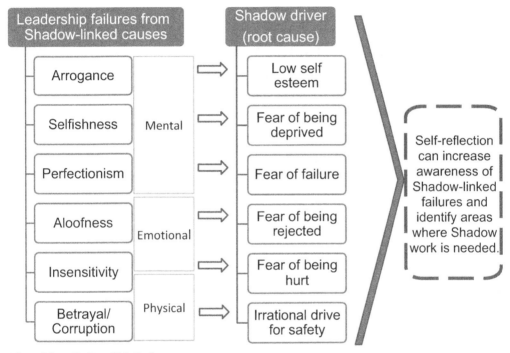

Adapted from Dr Ronald J. Burke

Self-centeredness is the underlying factor that ties together these six instances of failed leadership. Addressing self-centeredness is not always a rational process, as it can be deeply ingrained. This underscores the significance of the leader being genuinely motivated by a caring attitude towards the Collective, with a sense of duty to serve beyond self-interests. As a result, the leader is able to enhance relationships and build trust.

Here are some additional examples of root causes and their symptoms:

Oppression (root cause linked to unactualised emotional needs)

If a leader experienced oppression from his seniors during his earlier years, it may result in him replicating such behaviour one day when he occupies a senior position. This could result in the victimising of juniors, for the cycle to repeat itself. This action might be justified with the rationale "it also happened to me in my day." Tyranny raises its head as oppressive behaviour becomes the norm, with a view that juniors have not yet earned their right to respect.

Defensiveness (root cause linked to unactualised spiritual needs)

The fear of being exposed for having a derailed plan could trigger a self-righteous response in the leader, stemming from a fear of lacking direction or purpose. This may result in feelings of insecurity and isolation as the leader puts up a figurative defensive wall around himself.

Fears that extinguish leadership

There could also be a dormant Shadow. These are potential forces of the personality, which could be predispositions, inclinations and tendencies - whether known or unknown - which could manifest as the Shadow. These **potential forces are latent** but may be activated at any time.

In times of crisis, the Shadow of the Warrior Leader could manifest itself in the form of self-righteousness, with the leader consequently victimising his people. However, in times of non-crisis, the Shadow of the Steward Leader could result in excessive caretaking, weak or **Laissez-faire Leadership**. The French phrase laissez faire literally means 'allow to do', with the leader allowing the people to do as they choose. The understanding of leadership failures is compounded when there are the 'bad' people who fool us into believing they are 'good'. **Beware of the wolf in sheep's clothing.** Most people are honest and law-abiding citizens, concerned with contributing to society and living in a fair and just world. It is important to acknowledge that there may be a small number of individuals in a workplace who deviate from acceptable norms, act in a self-serving manner, have no conscience and lack empathy. These individuals can be challenging to manage and may even face dismissal due to serious misconduct. Unfortunately, they are often able to get away with misconduct and other anti-social behaviour. Often these people have no regard for fairness and equity.

A study conducted by the University of Washington revealed that a single negative team member can be the catalyst for a group's downward spiral. This gives credence to the idiom, "it takes one bad apple to spoil the barrel." Another study found that most respondents could pinpoint at least one 'bad apple' they had worked with who caused organisational dysfunction.

This type of person could be a psychopath, sociopath or a narcissist. They display a personality disorder rooted in lying, manipulation, deceit and other destructive traits. Forbes reports that up to 12% of CEOs exhibit psychopathic tendencies, which is a significantly higher percentage than the estimated 1% in the general population. The fact that the rate of psychopathic traits observed among corporate CEOs (15% to 20%) resembles that found among convicted criminals, as reported by the FBI, is worrisome.

The difference between a psychopath, sociopath and a narcissist:

- A psychopath possesses an egocentric and antisocial personality, showing no remorse for their actions, lacking empathy for others, and often exhibiting criminal tendencies.

- A sociopath displays asocial or antisocial behaviour or experiences antisocial personality disorder.

- A narcissist is extremely self-centered with an inflated sense of self-importance.

A breakdown of these differences is presented in the table below.

Characteristics	Psychopath	Sociopath	Narcissist
No empathy	√	√	√
No conscience or remorse	√	√	√
Egocentric	√	√	√
Manipulative	√	√	√
Controlling	√	√	
Violent	√	√	
Criminal	√		

Credit: Samaki Bilakichwa, C. Chiste 2022

Personal and Collective Unconscious

According to Jungian theory, the psyche consists of two complementary and opposite spheres: consciousness and unconsciousness. Consciousness represents a very small part of the psyche dominated by unconscious forces. Unconsciousness consists of a personal and a collective unconscious. The personal unconscious is all the forgotten, repressed, subliminally perceived psychic contents. Although consciousness cannot keep track of or store all your memories, the personal unconscious stores all forgotten or unpleasant psychic contents. The collective unconscious refers to the psychological legacy shared by all humans, which has been amassed over time through evolution. Within this realm lies the Jungian archetypes, which are universally present within our psychological heritage and endure through time. They can be a powerful way to achieve wholeness and a sense of connection, serving to free us from our self-centeredness and isolation. The unconscious consists of different layers of contents, ranging from the individual to the more collective, such as family, tribe, nation and ancestors.

Addressing emotional baggage that no longer serves is crucial for personal development. Jung believed that people sometimes deny the primitive and unadapted element of their own psyche and instead project it onto others. Many people in leadership positions hold closely onto their persona and tend to suppress the connection to their Shadow. To merely suppress the Shadow is as little of a remedy as beheading would be for a headache. Understanding the root cause is crucial to correct it. Daily life demands can often bring out the Shadow and its hidden motives, revealing other competing interests. If the Shadow is repressed and isolated from consciousness, it never gets corrected. Leadership theory is often developed under the assumption that the leader is equipped with goodwill and intellectual understanding to avoid mistakes. Research shows that leadership failures come from both psychological blockages and mistakes. In the case of blockages, by going within to carry out self-reflection a leader can address blockages to achieve self-actualisation. Incorporating our deeper understanding of the Shadow, we can now illustrate **this dark side of leadership** by recalling the diagram depicting the no Ownership vacuum (Figure 24) within the system.

Figure 35

Steward-Warrior Leadership Model:

No Ownership vacuum with Shadow consideration

Source: © C. Chiste 2021

Note: To illustrate the importance of Shadow observance, the Shadow is now included in the diagram above.

Even for the Steward-Warrior Leader who has self-actualised, continuous self-reflection is required. This is to ensure that the leader does not "lead from the Shadows". A Shadow-operating leader may resemble a Warrior Leader, but his lack of selflessness could result in a tyrannical Pseudo Warrior Leader. Similarly, a leader presenting himself as a Steward Leader but lacking concern for people is a weak Pseudo Steward Leader.

Figure 36

How the Shadow shows up for the leader

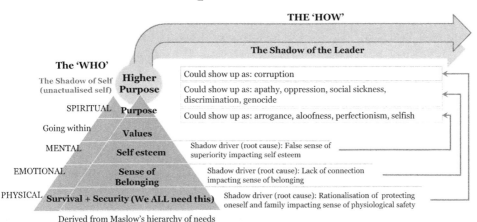

Source: © C. Chiste 2021

Leaders liberated from psychological blockages are **empowered** to effectively apply leadership theory. Jung describes this empowerment as follows:

"What does lie within our reach, however, is the change in individuals who have, or create for themselves, an opportunity to influence others of like mind.

*I do not mean by persuading or preaching – I am thinking, rather, of the well-known fact that anyone who has **insight into his own actions**, and has thus found access to the unconscious, involuntarily exercises an **influence on his environment**."*

LEADERSHIP EXERCISE: Putin vs Zelensky

Leaders are often judged and remembered by their legacy, which typically becomes clear years later, after their tenure has ended and the dust has settled. This is when the history books are written, and the impact of their leadership is assessed by future generations. A leader's legacy can be positive, negative or mixed, being shaped by their actions, decisions and the lasting changes they bring about during their time in power.

To analyse two contemporary leaders, we can examine two influential adversaries at the centre of world stage: Russian President Vladimir Putin and Ukrainian President Volodymyr Zelensky.

Take a moment and select the appropriate leadership dimensions which apply to each leader. Both leaders have shown warrior attributes of resilience and courageous action. Whilst it may be subjective, are you able to consider who is more of a Warrior Leader? Or a Steward-Warrior Leader? Perhaps a Pseudo Warrior Leader?

Are you ready to take the test?

The leader displays the following:

Authenticity		Total Ownership	
Relationship with the Collective (empowering, mutual expectations)		Resilience	
Inspirational influence (influence transformatively)	Steward Leader	Courageous Selfless Action	Warrior Leader
Voluntary Subordination		Accountability	
Ethics (responsible morality)		Communication (safety and vision)	
Selflessness (transcendental spirituality)		The above dimensions without authentic caring Selflessness, self-reflection*	Pseudo Warrior Leader
Communication (empowerment and vision)		**A leader has all the dimensions of both the Steward and Warrior Leader**	**Steward - Warrior Leader**
The above dimensions without authentic caring Selflessness & willingness to encourage independent thought	Pseudo Steward Leader		

* Awareness of actions and consequences, return to Voluntary Subordination post-crisis.

When it comes to a Pseudo Warrior-Steward Leader, his leadership intentions might have been positive, but he could have been negatively influenced or yielded to temptation. To understand how such a seemingly well-intentioned leader could become 'contaminated', the analogy of a container can be useful in the context of personal leadership and self-care. Here, the container symbolises oneself and its contents represent one's thoughts, emotions and experiences. The container analogy is relevant in terms of how we interact with the world.

A container is physically finite with a bounded space, with a clear distinction between inside and outside. The container is able to withstand adversity and uncertainty, enabling leadership to navigate change and disruption caused by external influence. However, the mind can also sometimes be a leaky container, when not properly sealed, allowing external influences to negatively impact the mind. This concept of the container can be explained on two levels. The first container relates to the individual, whereas the second enlarged container encompasses the group which the individual forms part of.

The First Level: Self-Leadership where the leader 'seals his container'. This specifically refers to preventing energy leakages from negative influences.

Figure 37
The sealed container

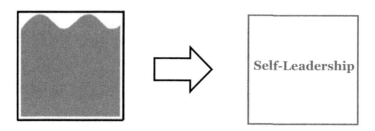

The first diagram above is a detailed depiction of a sealed container holding water, with the second diagram a simplification. The level of water represents the level of your mental energy and resilience, i.e. the leader holding space for himself.

Note: The more leaks the container has, the less water it will be able to hold.

*"**Self-Leadership** is a comprehensive self-influence perspective that concerns leading oneself toward performance of naturally motivating tasks,*

*as well as managing oneself to do work that must be done but is **not naturally motivating**."*

Charles C. Manz, University of Minnesota

According to Manz, self-leadership is an ongoing journey of self-discovery that requires consistent effort and commitment. The process involves several key components, including:

- Determining whether your goals are in alignment with your True Self.

- Being mentally tough and resilient in order to deal with challenges whilst in pursuit of your goals.

- Having self-awareness, being conscious of whether you are applying a fixed or growth mindset.

Before a leader can lead others, he needs to practice Self-Leadership. Metaphorically, before looking to enlarge the container and lead others, the leader must first **seal their own container** (Fig 40). This involves taking Ownership on a personal level, also referred to as personal Ownership, i.e., taking ownership of who you are, your personal purpose and the result.

Fundamentally, leadership concerns the leader's calling to serve beyond this personal level, i.e. the expansion beyond your personal container to also hold the space for the Collective. Using the container analogy, this expansion is represented graphically in the diagram that follows.

Figure 38

Enlarging the container to 'hold the space' for the Collective: Sealing the enlarged container

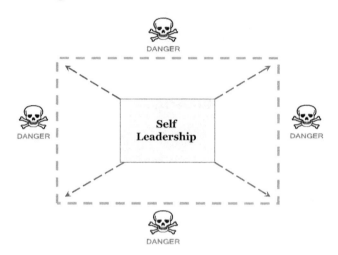

Note: Sealing the first container represents Self-Leadership (depicted by the inner shaded rectangle). This allows the leader to enlarge this container (represented by the enlarged rectangle depicted by the dashed lines) in order to hold the space for the Collective.

This enables the leader to provide safety and protection against external threats, creating space for the empowerment of the Collective towards a vision. The figure above shows the three facets that leaders need to be conscious of:

- leading themselves (depicted by the shaded rectangle);
- leading others (within the enlarged container – depicted by the dashed lined rectangle); and
- understanding the external environment (outside the enlarged container – depicted by the danger signs). In line with this concept of an enlarged container, Shankman and Allen state it in their book *Emotionally Intelligent Leadership*, leaders must be conscious of three fundamental facets of leadership:

1. Self.

   This concerns the leader's self-awareness.

2. Others.

   This could be people internal or external to the organisation.

3. Context.

   This pertains to the context in which leaders operate, which demands that they offer both safety and clarity in terms of the vision. It can also be seen as a systemic approach to understand how external factors affect a leader's ability to lead and stay true to their positive intentions.

Whilst self-actualisation is usually on top of Maslow's pyramid, Maslow later introduced the concept of self-transcendence. This results in peak experiences, where individuals transcend personal concerns to gain a higher perspective. Self-transcendence is a critical aspect of leadership. This is when the leader moves beyond self-interest to heed a calling to serve the Collective.

The statement, "You cannot give what you don't have" is obvious for material things. You cannot give money that you do not have. What people fail to understand about this statement is that it applies at every level of your being. Before you can lead people, you must first be able to lead yourself. The leader must first seal his own container. Once this is sealed, the leader can then address the second enlarged container which focuses on leading people and organisations. This concerns the HOW of effective leadership.

This enlargement provides a **sense of safety** for the Collective. This is built on trust, by way of shared values, interests and vision. In the days of Moshoeshoe, when groups were defined along tribal lines, being outside of the tribe meant being out of the safety of the tribe. For the hunter-gatherer, danger beyond the container could have taken the form of exposure to the harsh elements of the environment, hostile tribes or dangerous wild animals. Today, this concept of danger outside the container remains. In a business context, the danger could come from competitors, rivals or disruption of business. Within the container, your followers feel **safe** and have a sense of belonging. Think of a business leader, who in times of a recession needs to reassure employees that the organisation has the resources to see the downturn through. The leader plays a crucial role in shaping the interpretation of the organisation's financial performance, whether it's a profit or a loss. By providing a clear narrative, the leader sets the direction for servicing existing clients and pursuing new business opportunities.

Chapter 7
Safety along the Continuum

If an organisation is fear-driven and on the brink of collapse, the sense of safety will differ to that of an organisation coming off the back of a record profit. In this sense, safety can be thought of in terms of a continuum, with business as usual at the one end and a crisis situation at the other end.

There is no guarantee that a leader will be effective, despite the perceived level of skill. Other contributing factors may come into play. To better understand these factors, the aforementioned **systems thinking** approach can provide a perspective that emphasises the interconnectedness and interdependence of various components within a system. This approach allows for insight into how changes in one part of the system could have a knock-on effect throughout the entire system, helping to identify root causes of problems and develop effective solutions.

By adopting this comprehensive approach, leaders can make effective decisions that takes into account a wide range of variables, enabling them to avoid being one-dimensional and providing them with a well-informed frame of reference. Systems thinking can be integrated into leadership by taking into account relevant variables such as the leader, the Collective, communication, and culture, which are categorised based on the orientation of the Safety Continuum. The Systems Leadership Equation was formulated to recognise and take into account significant variables, and the equation is as follows:

$$\textit{Systems Leadership} = \frac{\overbrace{\textit{Leader Factor} + \textit{Collective} + \textit{Culture} + \textit{Communication}}^{\text{Non-leader variables within and external to organisation}}}{\textit{Orientation on Safety Continuum} * \theta}$$

Source: © C. Chiste 2022

Figure 39
The Safety Continuum

Crisis   **Safety Continuum**   Business as usual

(the "new" normal)

Source: C. Chiste 2021

The sense of safety can be viewed as a continuum, which spans from a sense of stability and peace at one end to a crisis-like environment during times of uncertainty and radical change at the other end. In a crisis-like scenario, fear may be induced by a perceived lack of control or a threat to one's well-being. Conversely, during times of stability, the potential for growth and progress may result in feelings of excitement or opportunity.

Crisis-like times	**Times of business as usual**
Generally, psychological safety allows people to feel safe, where they can collaborate, and problem solve together.	Psychological safety is a social condition where individuals freely express themselves, take risks and share ideas without fear. It cultivates trust, respect and open communication, fostering creativity, teamwork and problem-solving. Despite uncertainty, psychological safety is crucial for a supportive and inclusive environment. A universal pattern in social settings is the need to protect status/career.
During a crisis or an unwanted change, safety could encompass both a psychological and physiological aspect. The physiological pertains to the threat to survival or the potential threat to one's accustomed way of life. To counter this, the leader steps into the Warrior Leader to address the fear.	

"Adversity quickens the mind, awakens the spirit and strengthens the soul."

Lailah Gifty Akita

The introducer of the OODA Loop, Colonel Boyd, was a firm advocate that uncertainty is a precondition for mental and physical vitality. New possibilities often emerge when there is a discrepancy between the existing reality and our preconceived notions about it. To take advantage of opportunities without being consumed by fear, it is necessary to have a sense of safety.

Figure 40
The leader takes Ownership of the Safety Continuum

- Comfortable with complexity
- Openness to change
- Identify opportunities

By providing safety, the leader brings stability which also serves to build trust in the leader. Feeling safe in your environment enables a transition from basic survival mode thinking to a more lateral thinking approach.

Psychologist Shawn Achor suggests that a positive state of mind can improve performance by 31%, resulting in the discovery of opportunities and resolution of complex problems. A study at the University of Warwick showed that happy employees were 12% more productive than their unhappy colleagues. Furthermore, a meta-analysis of studies on positive psychology interventions found that such interventions generally improved work performance.

The leader can determine the most effective leadership approach by assessing the orientation on the Safety Continuum. When individuals are in survival mode, ensuring their physiological and psychological safety is crucial, which corresponds to the left end of the continuum. The goal is to create an environment where people are in flourish mode, which is situated on the right end of the continuum.

The positioning on the Ownership Continuum is guided by the Safety Continuum and its interaction within the wider leadership framework, as depicted below.

Figure 41

The Steward-Warrior Leadership Framework

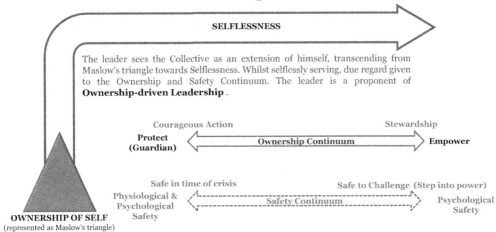

Source: © C. Chiste 2022

The diagram above illustrates the leader's selflessness, which manifests as a sincere concern for the Collective. The leader takes Ownership, in terms of Self, the mission and the result. Whilst undertaking the mission, the leader pays due regard to the Ownership Continuum and Safety Continuum to regulate behaviour.

Leadership in its 'pure' form

Simply put, leadership is about leading people to a better reality. The intended outcome of the leader and how this is achieved has been the subject of substantial research.

There are many reasons as to the means that people may have acquired leadership positions. Many so-called 'leaders' were appointed to leadership positions through questionable means, such as through political connections, nepotism or cadre deployment. Dubious sources of funding could mean that leaders are beholden to their donors and compelled to serve their interests.

Some of these leaders manipulate news with populist rhetoric to appear as saviours. Their intention is to win people over by telling people what they want to hear, regardless of the negative impact on ordinary citizens. An example is the British public relations company, Bell Pottinger's high profile White Monopoly Capital campaign. In 2016, Bell Pottinger ran a 'dirty campaign' in South Africa, exploiting racial tensions and spreading fake news. This was to benefit their client Oakbay Investments, a company controlled by the controversial and influential Gupta family who had questionable ties to the government of then President Zuma. The public outcry resulted in the bankruptcy of Bell Pottinger in 2017, who only a year earlier had recorded a strong revenue of GBP 27 million.

The key questions people may ask about the leader:

- What is the leader's real intention for leading?

- Is the leader focused on self-interest or a special interest group?

- More importantly, does the leader have my best interests at heart?

- Do I really buy into the leader as a person?

- Am I prepared to stand by the leader even in trying times?

A further question could be:

Does the leader generally lead by means of force, manipulation or by inspiration?

To gain a deeper understanding of this question, it's important to take into account the context surrounding it, which can provide a more complete and accurate depiction of the situation at hand.

In the hunter-gatherer days, the manipulation of information by means of technology and information did not exist.

The tribe's reliance on the leader to navigate them towards safety highlights the importance of a Warrior Leader. If the leader fails to provide this kind of guidance, it can result in the disintegration of the tribe due to fear and chaos. During that era, the role of a leader was to create a safe and secure environment for the tribe. Leaders had to go beyond relying on PR tactics and spin doctors, as they had to hold the space for the tribe. This involved cultivating a culture of mutual support, enhancing productivity, and aligning the tribe with a common vision. As a result, being a Warrior Leader was crucial in those times.

Leaders can achieve institutional holding both formally and informally. Formal measures are taken to provide assurance to individuals about job security and fair treatment through policies and procedures, while informal means are employed through the organisational culture.

My practical experience of this dimension from the military

Times of crisis

The leader is responsible to ensure both physiological and psychological safety through communication and by action. Given that I had recently completed my astro-navigation certification, this had positioned me to be selected as the navigator for the South African Navy Sailing team in an international competition called the Governor's Cup. My job was to ensure that we navigated safely by means of celestial bodies (stars, planets, sun), in the event the GPS failed. The Governor's Cup is an exciting 1700-mile summer ocean race from Cape Town to James Bay on St Helena Island. This is the island chosen by the British as the place of exile for Napoléon Bonaparte, after the Battle of Waterloo. The journey took us 11 days. However, halfway into the race I was awoken at 3am by our skipper as he shouted, *"All hands on deck! Everyone on the upper deck! Now!"* Adding to my abrupt awakening, I quickly realised that something was wrong when I found myself lying on the deckhead (ceiling) of my cabin, which was essentially 'upside down'.

Emerging from the sleeping quarters still half-asleep, I rushed to the stern of the yacht. My eyes were instantly drawn to the skipper, who was clutching the guardrails with all his might. His legs dangled precariously outside the vessel as the waves relentlessly crashed against him. Struggling for breath, he managed to rasp out a warning: *"Whatever you do, do not let go!"*

During those moments, a significant portion of our food supplies and crucial safety equipment were lost overboard. Looking to the bows of the yacht, which was now immersed underwater with the yacht almost perpendicular to the raging sea. I noticed the foresail filling with water, the more it filled it had the effect of sucking the yacht into the sea. The skipper decided to act fast. We were in the middle of the Atlantic Ocean with nobody else in sight. We were all alone and it was up to us to resolve this. The skipper shouted again for us to hold tight. He made his way to the fore of the ship with a knife, cutting the foresail loose. Immediately the yacht corrected itself and as a team we raised a new foresail. Throughout this ordeal the skipper's words and presence provided an assurance that we were safe.

Times of business as usual

The leader is responsible for ensuring psychological safety to inspire and empower people. We have all heard the statement that there is no such thing as a stupid question. This serves to make people feel safe to speak up without fear of judgment. This concerns the creation of an environment which is conducive to the raising of consciousness. During my time in banking, I was fortunate to work at two banks that placed an important focus on culture. In my first week at my second bank I was told, "We are a flat structure and a small team. There is no place to hide." This reminded me of the scene from the Wizard of Oz when Dorothy tells her dog, Toto, that she has a feeling they were no longer in Kansas. Despite feeling as if I was no longer in my comfort zone, I felt empowered and saw this as an opportunity for growth. The environment was geared towards results, with little time for politics or negativity.

In times of adversity, it's the leader's responsibility to **hold the space** for the organisation. This means thinking and communicating clearly, offering reassurance and fostering a culture of unity. Through actions and words, the leader can create a sense of stability and resilience that helps the organisation weather the storm and emerge stronger on the other side.

However, the ability to inspire is equally important. In fact, it could be regarded as a precondition. Depending on where the leader determines the orientation on the Safety Continuum, different needs would need to be prioritised.

In times of adversity, uncertainty and change, there are certain principles which apply to leadership. These principles do not provide solutions on a detailed basis. For example, they do not address company-specific issues such as capital adequacy or the need for vision setting work sessions.

Lessons on overcoming adversity from Shackleton's Endurance

Dr Dennis Perkins, a former US Marine, describes these principles as providing a 'leader's eye view' to capture the nature of the journey being experienced by the leader in times of adversity. Let us consider the saga of Sir Ernest Shackleton's misadventure in his attempt to become the first explorer to cross the Antarctic continent. Only 45 days after setting off on December 5, 1914, disaster struck. Shackleton's ship, *Endurance*, found itself trapped in ice with the entire crew stranded in the icy sea for 634 days.

The survival of the crew was not solely dependent on their determination or group unity, as they were faced with a major disruption when they became trapped in the ice. Shackleton's leadership had to encompass a **system thinking** approach, taking into consideration how all aspects of their situation were interconnected. By understanding the dynamics of this pivotal moment, Shackleton was able to create a sense of safety to seal the enlarged container and foster a determination to survive among the crew. An important lesson from this saga was that the principles which sustain you when you are on the limit of survival, could also be applied to any other challenges you may encounter in your life or business.

Figure 42

Safety Continuum and Consciousness Spectrum interplay: Understanding the concept of Teal Organisations

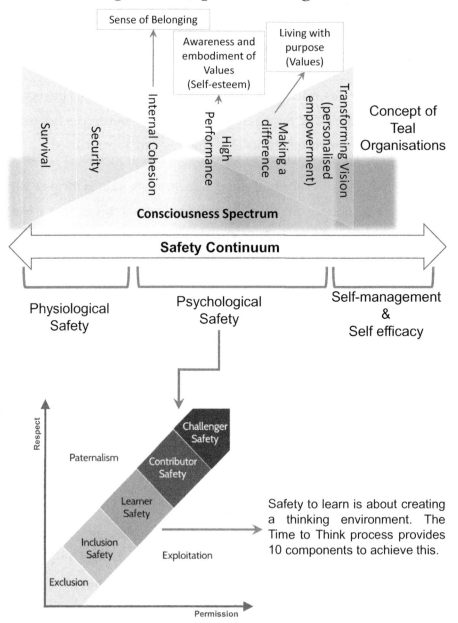

Dr Timothy Clark defines Psychological Safety as a condition in which people feel included (stage 1), safe to learn (stage 2), safe to contribute (stage 3) and safe to challenge the status quo (stage 4). However, in the context of this book, psychological safety pertains to the higher levels of Maslow's hierarchy, beyond basic physiological needs, as illustrated in Figure 45.

Challenging the status quo doesn't have to be confrontational. It can be approached positively through innovation and disrupting conventional thinking, without fear of being marginalised, embarrassed or punished. This approach not only encourages new ideas but also recognises the value of established methods. In a workplace setting, this translates to creating a safe space for diverse perspectives to be shared professionally. Combining the work of Clark's four stages of Psychological Safety and Nancy Kline's *Time to Think*, the path towards creating an empowering environment becomes clearer.

This path is placed into a logical sequence of stages starting with inclusion, with the second stage being 'Learner Safety'. The concept of a 'learner' is expanded in this book to include multiple aspects of learning, such as having a growth mindset that allows for continued personal development and a sense that all things are possible. To gain a better understanding of what makes a safe learning environment, the book delves into the ten components of Time to Think, providing an in-depth exploration of each.

On the right of the spectrum is the concept of a **Teal Organisation.** This refers to an organisational theory that enables workers to manage themselves and adapt as the organisation grows. Teal Organisations prioritise social and environmental impact over profit and create an environment for individuals to work towards a shared vision and purpose. This can be a meaningful platform for those called to serve the greater good. Similar to the concept of Ownership-driven Leadership, the focus is on self-management to empower individuals to take Ownership of their work and contribute in a way aligned with personal values, which is motivating for positive change. Teal Organisations provide a framework for individuals to work in an environment aligned with their values and make a meaningful impact. This concept was introduced in 2014 by Frederic Laloux. It builds on previous studies done by evolutionary psychologists including Jean Gebser, Clare W. Graves, Don Edward Beck, Chris Cowan and Ken Wilber. Their research explored the stages of human development and the impact on consciousness.

A real-life example of participative management

In Ricardo Semler's book Maverick, he shares that upon assuming control of the family engineering firm, he immediately let go of 60% of the top management on his first day. He enabled unprecedented worker involvement in the business, including worker-selected management. Semler's philosophy emphasised trust, transparency and a focus on results over rules. This people-centric approach to leadership resulted in the firm being dubbed "**the world's most unusual workplace**".

The context of your organisation plays a crucial role in deciding how you adopt this leadership approach. The important aspect is to tailor principles to suit the unique requirements of your organisation. He believed that it is vital to empower employees to ensure growth and innovation. To generate innovative ideas, it is vital to have an environment that fosters creativity.

Creating an environment conducive to creative and critical thinking

The Partners for Possibility (PfP) Program was initiated in South Africa to promote active citizenship in order to facilitate change leadership in schools. Many of the schools are under resourced with many social issues in economically challenged areas. The programme pairs business leaders with school principals as part of a one-year commitment to active citizenship. During my term as a Business Leader on the programme, we utilised the *Time to Think* methodology to facilitate the creation of a thinking environment. Kline lists ten behaviours that generate the finest thinking. As leaders we must be aware that our actions set the tightness of the container. This enables a thinking environment. These ten components enable creativity and innovation, generating open mindedness towards each other to harness safety and trust. It is from the quality of thinking that people make their best decisions.

A brief overview of the ten *Time to Think* components:

1. Attention	Attention is to be regarded as an act of creation. When you listen, this must be done with palpable respect and genuine interest, without interruption.
2. Equality	Treating each other as equal thinkers to ensure that everyone feels that their thoughts matter. This can be achieved by keeping boundaries and agreements. Even though you may have power and authority over individuals, you value their time and opinions.
3. Ease	Ease frees from stress, aiding clear thinking for better decision-making and cognitive performance.
4. Appreciation	The human mind works best in the presence of appreciation. For every critic there should be at least five compliments, i.e. a ratio of 5:1.
5. Encouragement	Focusing only internally can be counter-productive as it can keep the attention on each other. Giving encouragement to move beyond internal competition directs the focus externally.
6. Feelings	Allow sufficient emotional release to restore thinking. This is to avoid unexpressed feelings as they can inhibit good thinking. By people showing their feelings, we relax and welcome them, thus allowing good thinking to resume.
7. Information	Supplying the facts, recognising social context to dismantle denialism, which is often the first step to independent thinking. Facing what we have been avoiding or denying results in better thinking.
8. Diversity	Diverse groups bring varied perspectives, increasing potential for impactful thinking. Embracing diversity and respecting everyone's voice drives innovation and success.
9. Incisive Questions	Asking incisive questions is a valuable coaching technique. It can be used to identify and question untrue assumptions that a person may have about themselves. This assists to see a new perspective and declutter the minds.

10. Place	The physical environment affirms our importance, allowing us to think more clearly and boldly.
	As is the case with our bodies, when cared for and respected, our thinking improves. Thinking environments are places that say to people, "You matter."

When leaders hold the space, they create a safe and supportive environment where these ten components can thrive. For example, the leader must pay full attention to the individual or group he is leading to ensure that everyone's ideas and thoughts are heard and valued (component 1: attention). The leader must also ensure that everyone has an equal opportunity to contribute, with diverse perspectives respected (components 2 and 8: equality and diversity). The leader should encourage and appreciate his team's ideas, creating an atmosphere of positive reinforcement (components 4 and 5: appreciation and encouragement). The leader should also ask incisive questions to promote critical thinking and help the team arrive at insightful solutions (component 9: incisive questions).

Holding the Space

By the leader holding the space, it creates an environment that says to people:

"I am here to listen, support and guide you. I trust that you are capable of making your own decisions."

Leadership models often overlook the holding aspect of leadership, an obscure and seldom celebrated facet, with most of the focus placed on vision. However, it is no less important. Drawing upon the earlier analogy of a container of water. If this container were to be transported, it is critical to have a destination in mind (vision). However, if the container is leaky, the container will arrive empty. Leadership holding addresses these possible leakages.

In times of crisis, having no leaks in the container becomes even more important. When the leader is able to hold the space, people feel a measure of safety. This enables more expansive thinking to take place in which new ideas and solutions emerge.

However, when the leader cannot hold the space, this fuels disharmony as the environment is not conducive for connectedness. This lack of safety and mutual support can become a breeding ground for anxiety, anger and fragmentation. In a study of BP's response to the Deepwater Horizon oil spill in the Gulf of Mexico carried out by Professor Jennifer Petriglieri from INSEAD, there were found to be both positive and negative outcomes.

The study found that despite BP uniformly tasking their internal leaders to resolve the crisis to ensure recovery, the results yielded from their internal leaders could not have been more different. Some employees lost faith in the company and in its leaders, while others became highly motivated, doubling their efforts and commitment. What was the difference between these two polar opposite groups?

The employees who doubled their efforts and commitment, despite the stress, had hands-on leaders who worked closely with them through the adversity. These leaders were perceived to be more informative and provided reassurance on the company's integrity and long-term viability.

However, the employees who lost faith were those whose leaders were not seen to be standing by their side to reassure them, being exposed only to their leader's upbeat messages. These leaders maintained a hands-off approach even during the heat of the crisis. The study concluded that a leader who holds the space during a crisis is more effective than one who only gives verbal reassurance.

The pioneering British psychoanalyst Donald Winnicott observed that, for healthy growth in children, holding was necessary. Holding is a critical component of children's development, providing the stability and security needed to navigate the challenges of the inner and social worlds. By understanding the importance of holding, caregivers and parents can create a nurturing environment that supports children's healthy growth and development. In the process, children also develop their self-esteem and a healthy regard not only for abilities, but also limitations.

This approach enhances self-awareness and mental resilience, enabling the enduring of challenges while remaining hopeful. As noted by Winnicott, providing a holding environment doesn't mean sheltering children from the harshness of reality, but rather exposing them to it in small, manageable doses. Effective parents offer bite-size proportions of distress to their children, shielding them from excessive exposure while still instilling a sense of reality. The optimal holding environment is created by parents who are:

- Available but not demanding
- Reassuring but not intrusive
- Responsive but not reactive
- Present even if not perfect.

These actions were found to create an environment where children felt comfortable and curious to take on challenges, experiencing mental growth in the process. This helped children to find words to name their different experiences, be it positive or negative, whilst finding ways to manage them. The children who experienced being held in this way tended to develop greater sociability and independence as they grew up, fostering a sense of empowerment and feeling in control of their lives. Holding the space does not only make people more comfortable and courageous, but it also helps develop them. That was the major insight Winnicott observed.

Similarly, the leader needs to hold the space for the people. This fosters psychological safety for personal growth and development. Additionally, in challenging situations, it offers a feeling of support and reassurance, knowing that they are not facing difficulties alone.

Leadership effectiveness variables along the Safety Continuum:

Leaders must also consider non-leader variables in the broader system, beyond just applying leadership principles. Although the focus in this book has been primarily on the leader, there are a number of other variables to consider. It's important to acknowledge that there may be factors beyond the leader's control that contribute to their lack of effectiveness.

The Systems Leadership Equation highlights important non-leader variables for effective leadership, these include the Collective, culture, communication and the orientation on the Safety Continuum.

$$Systems\ Leadership = \frac{\overbrace{Leader\ Factor + Collective + Culture + Communication}^{\text{Non-leader variables within and external to organisation}}}{Orientation\ on\ Safety\ Continuum * \Theta}$$

The five key variables are expanded upon below:

Variable 1: The Leader

The Leader Factor refers to how a leader's positive intentions and effectiveness are perceived. This variable can be evaluated from two perspectives: the perception of those who have limited information and those who have access to behind-the-scenes knowledge. Research shows the primary reason for leadership failures is due to either leadership mistakes or psychological blockages. Mistakes can be limited by the leader's assessment of the organisation's position on the Safety Continuum which in turn informs him of the orientation on the Ownership Continuum. This ultimately guides the choice of leadership style. In order to address psychological blockages, continued raising of self-awareness is required. However, regardless of which style the leader adopts, he must manage himself on two distinct levels: Self-Leadership and Organisational Leadership.

Note: Chapters 2-6 essentially relate to this variable, which primarily concerns the HOW of leadership and Shadow management.

The first container: Self-Leadership

Self-Leadership focuses on personal Ownership, in relation to who you are, your personal mission and your result. Regular self-reflection is necessary to prevent being triggered. This is Shadow management which involves: self-reflection, root cause analysis to determine whether a leadership failure is linked to a psychological blockage or a mistake, alignment of the three Selfs in order to practice Authentic Leadership.

The second enlarged container: Organisational Leadership

This concerns the leader's ability to hold the space for the people within the organisation. This requires the ability to orientate along the Ownership Continuum to adapt to the situation. To ensure a comprehensive understanding of the context, it's essential to consider external factors beyond the boundaries of the organisation. This can be achieved by applying a systems thinking approach that takes into account the various variables that impact the organisation. Such an approach can be seen as a third level of leadership, in addition to Self-Leadership and Organisational Leadership. However, as organisations become more interconnected, the container analogy should not be seen as a closed system. Rather, this approach should inform leaders about the scope of their influence and help them to hold the space. This, in turn, ensures psychological safety and fosters a culture of innovation and growth.

In times of business as usual

Leaders offer institutional support by:

- Fostering a culture of shared purpose

- Establishing a robust culture.

Leaders not only establish the structure with a strong culture, but also strengthen with policies and procedures that promote job security and equity. This involves promoting collective consultation and Shared Ownership.

In times of crisis

There are times when the urgency of the circumstance dictates that the leader bypasses the conventional decision-making process. This is facilitated by the Collective supporting the leader based on the trust built up. However, this support is on the proviso that the leader's non-consensus approach is temporary and in the best interests of the Collective.

Total Ownership by the leader is temporary. The leader's intention is to bring order and stability to ensure safety is an essential trait to have in times of crisis. Once the crisis is over, Shared Ownership is to be restored.

The leader's actions are in the best interests of the Collective. During a crisis, the leader motivates people to unite and adapt to new challenges. The leader may likely need to act in a bold manner to address an urgent issue to restore a sense of holding.

Providing institutional support can win people over as it taps into their primal need for survival. For a national leader, institutional holding transcends politics. People remember how they were treated during vulnerable times, particularly by those in power. We remember how our institutions, managers and peers held us through a crisis — or failed to.

We also see the consequences of institutions who failed to provide holding. The leader who fails to provide holding, runs the risk of any expressions of sympathy and understanding appearing unconvincing. It is tempting for a leader to blindly assume Command and Control in a crisis, no matter how honourable the intention may be.

However, for the Steward-Warrior Leader this action can be described as "selflessly assuming temporary Command and Control with the interest of the Collective at heart". Effective leadership demands the courage to take action when facing danger. However, it's important for a leader to assess the situation carefully and determine the appropriate response to address the threat and ensure the safety of those involved. By striking a balance between courageous action and prudent evaluation, a leader can demonstrate the ability to take decisive action when necessary. Creating a holding space means providing a safe environment where individuals can express their concerns and feel confident in their ability to overcome challenges. For example, if the Collective is facing an economic downturn, the leader will likely need to make difficult decisions in terms of downsizing or restructuring. The leader must communicate clearly and transparently with the organisation about the situation and the reasons behind the decision. This could include staff briefings, providing one-on-one coaching sessions or soliciting feedback. The key is to balance courage with empathy and sensitivity to the needs of the team. The leader must be willing to make tough decisions, but also be mindful of the impact on the individuals involved.

By holding the space and directing the Collective through the challenge, the leader can help the team emerge stronger and more resilient. This entails providing assistance and understanding to individuals facing emotional or professional struggles, while also acknowledging and celebrating achievements and victories throughout the journey. According to Professor Gianpiero Petriglieri, of INSEAD, the leader whose vision is typically the most compelling and enduring, is not the leader who started from a vision. Rather it was the leader who started with a sincere concern for the people. As the leader holds the space for the Collective during the period of transition, a vision tends to emerge. The leader's vision has the potential to captivate and inspire us, leaving a lasting impression. However, it is the leader's ability to empower and uplift us that truly makes a meaningful impact. Their influence goes beyond mere captivation, enabling us to reach new heights and unleash our full potential.

The following variables relate to non-leader variables, the robustness of which contribute to leadership effectiveness.

Variable 2: The Collective

While leaders bear ultimate accountability for the success of the organisation, it is crucial to recognise that the outcome of any endeavor is ultimately determined by the individuals they lead. There may be times that despite the leader's best efforts, some people may refuse to be led. The leader cannot lead if there are no followers. Just as there is an expectation placed upon the leader 'to lead', there is also an expectation from the leader that the people do their part. Jim Collins in his book *Good to Great*, refers to this concept as "getting the right people on the bus". It is important to emphasise that Ownership is a shared responsibility. The leader should not strive for forced compliance and conformity. Leadership effectiveness is also dependent on the Collective's responsiveness in taking Ownership.

In times of business as usual

During business as usual, effective leadership involves empowering individuals to operate within a framework of competence, established through a mutual agreement between the leader and their followers, i.e. Covenantal Relationship.

The leader sets clear expectations for the organisation's deliverables while offering the necessary support and resources to foster success. This balance of accountability and support creates an environment where individuals can thrive and contribute to the organisation's overall achievements.

However, Covenantal Relationships are not just the responsibility of the leader - the Collective also has a critical role to play. Each team member must take Ownership and be accountable for their contribution. This entails fostering strong collaboration with team members, actively seeking opportunities for growth and being proactive in addressing any challenges that arise. By embracing a collective approach and consistently working towards improvement, people can effectively achieve their shared objectives and cultivate an environment rooted in trust and a commitment to excellence. For example, a leader might empower a team member to take the lead on a project that aligns with their expertise and interests. The leader provides guidance and resources as needed, but also trusts team members to make decisions and take risks within the agreed-upon framework.

In times of crisis

In 2005 Salvatore Maddi emphasised the importance of **human connection** for mental resilience and hardiness, arguing that it is a crucial factor in individuals who bounce back and resist stress. Maddi suggested that the success of a self-help group lies, in part, in the power of belonging and connectedness which being a member of a community provides. According to this theory, social support plays a vital role in protecting people from the adverse effects of stress. Studies have indicated that a cohesive team can act as a support system for colleagues who may be struggling to cope with a persistent issue. This principle is the foundation of self-help groups, which aid in mental recovery, such as the well-known Alcoholics Anonymous (AA). Paradoxically, the overwhelming anguish of grief or suffering often results in individuals isolating themselves and seek solace within their own personal sanctuary. Nonetheless, it is important to acknowledge that seeking support from people is fundamental in navigating through loss. Finding solace in the presence of those who truly care can bring immense comfort.

Additionally, when individuals find themselves in vulnerable situations, it becomes imperative for both the state and community to extend some form of emotional and financial assistance, which may encompass various forms of aid such as social grants.

Another important consideration is that of trust in the leader's ability to resolve the crisis. A crisis has the tendency to disrupt the status quo. This means that the application of the leadership dimension, Covenantal Relationship, may change considerably in times of crisis specifically in terms of mutual expectations. The nature of this adjusted application is likely to involve a measure of discomfort for the Collective.

Variable 3: Communication

Effective leadership communication in an organisation serves the purpose of **inspiring, informing or persuading** in order to **influence** its functions. To be effective, the leader must be mindful of communicating a message that serves the intended purpose. The leader's proficiency in communicating the vision effectively inspires Ownership, facilitating the necessary focus of energy. Conversely, the leader must gather information about people's needs, concerns, and sentiments through ethical means, including direct and indirect methods.

In times of business as usual

A leader who communicates empowerment and reassurance fosters psychological safety, encouraging Shared Ownership.

In times of crisis

Communication needs to be frequent and brief. The information about the crisis should include a current update and a clear direction, along with providing support, clarity and guidance.

Variable 4: Culture

Deloitte's research reveals that 94% of executives consider a unique corporate culture to be crucial for success. The success or failure of an organisation could depend on its culture, which is primarily shaped by its values. A strong and durable organisation is formed when there are shared values, and the vision, ethical standards and accountability is clearly defined. Nevertheless, a pragmatic policy should also be implemented to support a healthy culture and facilitate the achievement of the organisation's mission.

In times of business as usual

The leader should cultivate a work environment that empowers initiative, free from fear of falling short of desired results. Encouraging creative and critical thinking requires the leader to establish psychological safety. A positive workplace includes simple gestures like greeting colleagues, offering compliments and providing support during challenging times. Our brains possess mirror neurons that imitate the actions we observe from people around us. This phenomenon was evidenced in a study conducted by Duke University, where 222 out of 328 participants who watched a 3-minute video of yawning were **contagiously influenced** and yawned at least once. This study underscores the power of positive behaviour to influence people. By modelling it, we create a more collaborative work environment.

In times of crisis

Having contingencies, structures and routines is an effective way to maintain order during a crisis. This provides a sense of continuity within your container.

Variable 5: Orientation along the Safety Continuum

The Safety Continuum concerns the leader's understanding of:

- The current sense of safety: The present level of safety is denoted by the orientation on the Safety Continuum, which impacts all other variables. The Safety Continuum ranges from 'Safe' to 'Not Safe'.

- Any **potential risks** which could pose a threat: To facilitate the leader in ensuring safety and mitigating risk, the leader needs to identify internal threats within the 'enlarged container' and external threats beyond this container. This is represented by Greek symbol theta, Θ, commonly used in mathematics and science to represent an unknown quantity or variable.

While this book provides leaders with dimensions for both challenging crisis-like scenarios and routine situations, individuals tend to have a natural disposition towards one. For instance, Musk is viewed as a Wartime CEO, as described by Horowitz, inclined towards crisis-like scenarios.

A Strategic Inflection Point:
The indicator that continuing with business as usual is Not Safe

Elon Musk ✓
@elonmusk

If a severe global recession were to dry up capital availability / liquidity while SpaceX was losing billions on Starlink & Starship, then bankruptcy, while still unlikely, is not impossible.

GM & Chrysler went BK last recession.

"Only the paranoid survive." – Grove

10:21 PM · Nov 30, 2021

♡ 14.1K   💬 964   ↑ Share this Tweet

Tweet your reply

Source: Twitter

This tweet sums up Musk's approach during an inflection point. In October 2022, he completed **one of the largest tech acquisitions of all time**, purchasing Twitter for USD 44 billion.

What is an inflection point? In mathematical terms, an **inflection point** is reached when the sign of the slope's rate of change, which is known as the 'second derivative', switches from positive to negative. In physical terms, it is the point where a curve changes from convex to concave, or vice versa. As illustrated in the diagram, it is the point at which a curve stops curving one way and starts curving the other way.

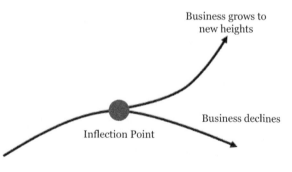

Business grows to new heights

Business declines

Inflection Point

Source: Andrew Grove, co-founder of Intel

An inflection point in the business world arises when the original strategy has failed significantly, compelling the need for a new one. Such a situation often arises when there are dramatic changes in the business environment. However, emotions can impede the necessary drastic action, despite the recognition of its urgency. Failing to navigate an inflection point could result in a rapid decline in your business after passing the peak. It is often around an inflection point that leadership realise that something is different, i.e. business is no longer operating as usual. A case in point being Intel, who for years had dominated the microchip market. This was until Japanese firms started making better quality memory chips, at a cheaper price. Consequently, many American memory chip companies went bankrupt in the mid-1980s. A 'strategic inflection point' had arrived. However, for Intel, the company well known for being the inventor of the world's first successful microprocessor, this would signal a strategic profitable turnaround.

Intel's loss of global dominance in the microchip market did not prevent them from achieving significant business success. Instead, their inflection point led them to secure their largest customer product base in a different market. This achievement was mainly due to their success in the personal computer market, resulting in a remarkable turnaround for the company. Consequently, *Time* magazine placed Intel CEO, Grove, on their cover choosing him as Man of the Year for 1997. In his book, *Only the Paranoid Survive*, Grove explains how companies, who for generations had a no-layoff policy, during a strategic inflection point were compelled to layoff thousands. He makes the point of the need to take Ownership, when he stated:

"Your career is literally your business. You own it as the sole proprietor. You have one employee: yourself. You are in competition with millions of similar businesses: millions of other employees all over the world.

*You need to accept **ownership** of your career, your skills and the timing of your moves.*

*It is **your responsibility to protect** this personal business of yours from harm and to position it to benefit from the changes in the environment. Nobody else can do that for you."*

Systems thinking leadership effectiveness variables summary: Crisis vs business as usual approach comparison

Leadership effectiveness is typically determined by analysing the leader's actions, often ignoring crucial non-leader variables which could have an impact. The summary of these variables is presented below:

Variable	Orientation on Safety Continuum	
	Crisis	**Business as usual (non-crisis)** The 'new' normal, can be crisis-like at times.
Leader	Is the leader prepared to take bold steps which may be unpopular in order to ensure safety of the Collective?	Does the leader make people feel included? Does the leader inspire people to grow and be more? Does the leader encourage people to participate regarding issues which impact them? Does the leader enable the people to provide feedback to challenge the status quo?
Collective	Do people trust the leader to resolve the crisis?	Do people commit to the Covenantal Relationship with their leader? There needs to be clarity on mutual expectations of both the leader and the people, and the commitment to deliver. Do the people buy into the leader's vision?
Communication	Does the leader communicate effectively? In times of crisis, people need to know they will be safe and that there is a plan. Information should be brief and regular.	Does the leader communicate the vision in a motivating and inspiring way?
Culture	Do people look out for each other? Is there a sense of community?	Do people have shared values? Do the people act without fear of being belittled or ostracised if they make a mistake?

Revisiting the container analogy with a deeper understanding of systems:

The following expanded conceptualisation is presented.

Container analogy Useful for outlining the ambit of concern: influence and holding space (safety)	Systems thinking Useful for analysing: complexity and consequence of action	Conceptual expansion: Container analogy vs systems analogy
First level Self Leadership	First order	**The leader** The concept of sealing the container expands to view the leader as a system. **Internal:** • Care-driven intention, i.e. **Batho Pele.** • Shadow management, i.e. Own who you are. **External:** • Understanding and applying the HOW of leadership, i.e. Own the mission. Own the result. Whilst ensuring no Ownership vacuum.
Second level	Second order	**Organisation: internal** The concept of the enlarged container is viewed as non-leader variables within the organisational system.
Third level DANGER DANGER DANGER DANGER	Third order	**Organisation: external** This concerns the variables beyond the enlarged container to provide context (threats, competition), i.e. the non-leader variables in the broader system, being external to the organisational system.

Ubuntu emphasises 'seeing' the interconnectedness of all humanity, this includes the people seeing the leader's presence, facilitating a strong connection or 'link' between the leader and people in different systems. The notion of **Isithunzi** takes this view of presence to the next level, almost like leadership presence 'on steroids'.

The cogs in the 'leadership engine'

For an engine to function, it requires all of its components. Gears, consisting of wheels with interlocking tiny teeth called cogs, are crucial in turning the wheels and powering the engine. Every cog is essential to that engine.

Gareth Morgan's *Images of Organization* suggests that organisations can be compared to machines. According to the machine metaphor, organisations are closed systems, with inputs, internal processes and outcomes. Not dissimilar to the enlarged container analogy presented in this book. Each component of the organisation fits together intentionally, much like cogs in an engine, underscoring the importance of standardising approaches and operations to attain maximum production efficiency.

Frederick Taylor (1856–1915), known as the *Father of Scientific Management,* introduced scientific management concepts which supported the view of organisations as closed systems. As systems become increasingly intricate and interconnected, this has become less the case. This is connected to the concept of Systems Leadership mentioned earlier, which emphasises the need to understand the broader system in which the organisation operates. The Steward-Warrior Leadership dimensions can also be seen as cogs. They are the competencies and attributes leaders employ, day in and day out, much like an engine being called upon to perform whenever required. This is the HOW of leadership. Unfortunately, the term cog is sometimes used when someone feels they have a small role to play, they might say, "I'm just a cog in the system." However, the true definition of the term cog is a "small, but instrumental part of the whole".

The Ownership Continuum with the full range of Steward-Warrior Leadership dimensions and foundational principles are presented in the diagram that follows.

Figure 43

The Full Range of Ownership-driven Leadership dimensions:
Detailed leadership dimensions and foundation along the continuum

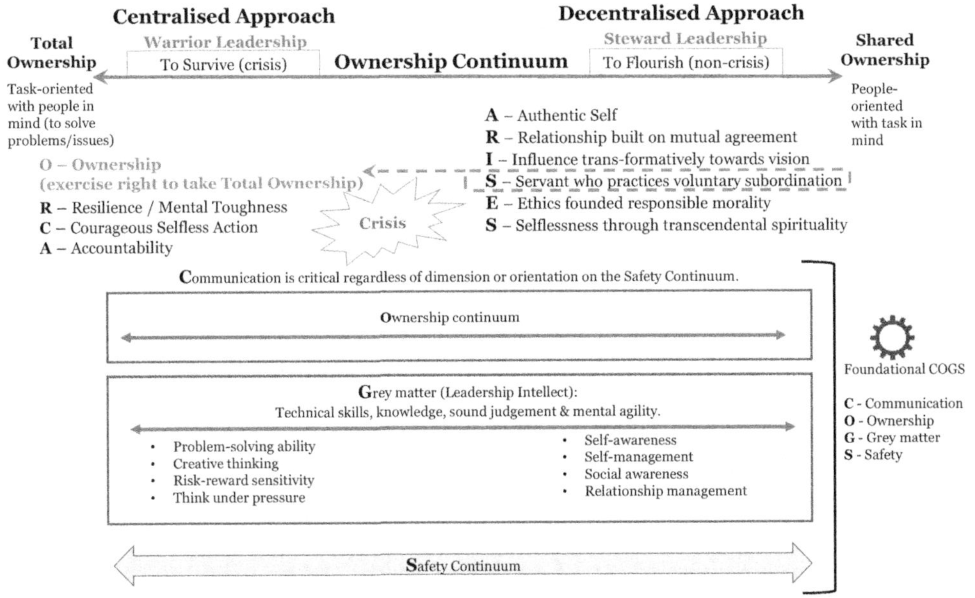

Source: © C. Chiste 2021

A **simplified depiction** of the above diagram is presented in Figure 44. Note: The foundational principles form the acronym COGS.

The Warrior Leader assumes Total Ownership, whilst being resilient and courageous, with mindfulness of action ever-present. Acting in the interests of the people is not a blank cheque; accountability is enhanced by considering unintended consequences through systems thinking.

The term **COG** in this context is not to be confused with Clausewitz's important concept of COG, which relates to Centre of Gravity, in his native German referred to as *Schwerpunkt*. This is the hub of all power and movement on which everything depends. Similar to the concept of Pareto's 80-20 principle, which asserts that 80% of outcomes (or outputs) result from 20% of all causes (or inputs) for any given event. In business this resonates with the words of Seneca: "A good man will not waste himself upon mean and discreditable work or be busy merely for the sake of being busy."

The following model illustrates how the Steward and Warrior dimensions interact as the safety orientation shifts, serving to provide a simple conceptual model of the Ownership-driven Leadership approach.

Figure 44
The Full Range of Ownership-driven Leadership dimensions:
Conceptual model of leadership dimensions and foundation

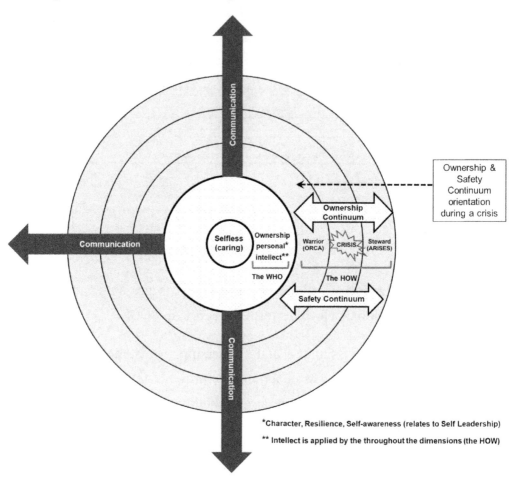

Source: © C. Chiste 2022

Note: Communication is crucial for all the dimensions, with due regard to the orientation on the Safety Continuum.

When implementing the Warrior Leadership dimensions, the Steward Leadership dimensions remain applicable, the only exception being the relinquishing of Voluntary Subordination. Regardless of which dimension is used in the approach, the leader's actions are motivated by care. During a crisis, leadership requires a hands-on approach, as individuals seek guidance and comfort from the leader. If the leader shows fear and anxiety, this emotion may spread throughout the team, but exhibiting character, courage and resilience creates a sense of safety.

To aid in remembering and applying this information, we see the ten dimensions of the Steward-Warrior Leader form the acronym ORCA ARISES.

O
R
C
A

A
R
I
S
E
S

Safety

This ORCA ARISES framework is constructed upon core principles, akin to interconnected cogs, encompassing robust Communication, understanding of the required orinetation on the Ownership continuum, intellectual acumen (Grey matter), and a focus on Safety. As previously mentioned, these elements combine to form the acronym COGS, representing the essential components of this foundation.

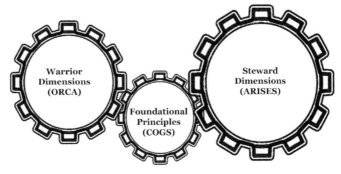

Warrior Dimensions (ORCA)

Foundational Principles (COGS)

Steward Dimensions (ARISES)

However, the nature and the application of these foundational principles will differ considerably depending on orientation on the Safety continuum.

Warrior Leadership in a nutshell

In Chapter 1 we took a cold, hard look at the harsh reality we find ourselves in today. Whether we realise it or not, we are being confronted with potential threats on multiple fronts.

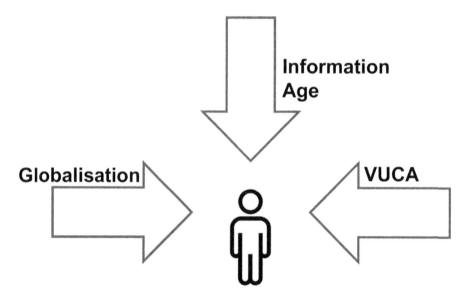

Humanity finds itself surrounded by multiple potential threats

Confronting potential threats on multiple fronts creates complexity as the leader must address multiple issues simultaneously, prioritising and allocating resources while balancing conflicting objectives. Interconnected threats may compound complexity, requiring a **systemic problem-solving approach**. Leaders need to be aware that this level of complexity means that the leader may not always be able to readily make sense of every situation. This requires an accurate assessment of the orientation on the Safety Continuum. It may tend towards Not Safe, even though the potential threat may not actually occur.

Assuming the leader is of sound character, resilient, competent and has common sense (intellect), the leader's selfless intention to serve can act as a North Star. This is the constant which can be relied upon to provide direction in a world of change and confusion.

Own the result:

Taking Ownership as a leader is crucial, regardless of the outcome. Whether succeeding, failing or failing catastrophically, accountability for your role as a leader by 'owning' the result is essential for effective leadership.

Are you inspiring an Ownership-driven life?

The world we live in is becoming increasingly complex, with organisations structured around a leader assuming a Command and Control approach often ineffective. By empowering your people there is synergy with everyone having the opportunity to be a leader in their own right. Submarine commander David Marquet refers to this principle as the Leader-Leader model, as opposed to the conventional Leader-Follower model. This model proved effective in the context of a high-risk environment, where people operate within a confined space and where everyone's contribution could make or break the mission.

Resilience

Mental resilience and a positive mental attitude play a key role in enduring challenges, enabling you to hold the space for those you lead. General George C. Marshall commented:

"When conditions are difficult, the command is depressed, and everyone seems critical and pessimistic, you must be especially cheerful and optimistic."

Courageous Selfless Action

While VUCA may be our current reality, this does not mean that we in a constant state of crisis. However, in situations where our way of life or existence is under threat, bold and decisive action needs to be taken to eliminate the threat and restore safety. Similar to the days of the classical warrior-leader, King Shaka, when great responsibility was placed on the leader to ensure the safety and survival of the tribe.

Accountability

The safety of the tribe rests on the leader's shoulders, requiring him to assume control and eliminate threats, while remaining accountable for the potential consequences of his actions.

There may be moments when the leader's decisions are met with resistance, despite the best intention to address a threat. Such scenarios could negatively impact the leader's professional advancement, even risking the end of his career. Conversely, playing it too safe carries the risk of ineffectiveness and irrelevance. General Marshall's words about a leader's willingness to sacrifice self for the common good resonates in this context. Understanding the potential consequence of action assists in navigating the challenges of decision-making. As a leader, it is essential to assess the effectiveness of your communication to ensure that people are aware of your intention. Equally important is actively listening to the voices and concerns of those you lead. Active listening is vital for understanding and trust.

King Shaka took charge to eliminate threats whilst building a strong sense of identity amongst the Zulu nation.

This sketch is believed to be the only life sketch of Shaka, attributed to trader James King. It appeared in Nathanial Isaacs' *Travels and Adventures in Eastern Africa* published in 1836.

Communication

Effective communication is crucial in both normal and adverse situations. During adversity, to be effective your message needs to be communicated frequently and briefly. People seek the truth and reassurance, although guarantees may be limited. As mentioned, people want to feel heard, with Mandela said to go over and beyond this, with those who were in his company saying he made them feel 'seen, heard and loved'.

Do your people feel safe?

Safety

Ensuring safety relies heavily on the leader's communication and actions.

Enabling the organisational champion

The Warrior Leader prioritises the safety of the people, perceiving his role as that of a guardian. In contrast, the Steward Leader's ultimate intention involves empowering people towards Shared Ownership.

The Steward Leader empowers people to become champions in their own right by living an Ownership-driven life. In his book "*Organizational Champions: How to Develop Passionate Change Agents at Every Level*," Mike Thompson defines an organisational champion as someone who commits themselves to their organisation's success through agility, creativity and honesty. This commitment is demonstrated through an unwavering dedication, having the ability to make a significant impact on the organisation. These champions are unafraid to make bold decisions that benefit not only their organisation but also the broader world. They prioritise long-term goals over immediate results and performance, enabling their organisation to evolve and maintain valuable relationships. In this regard, the Steward-Warrior Leader can be seen as an enabler of **organisational champions.**

This long-term view also helps their organisation evolve to meet future needs and maintain relationships. Meaning that they are not just looking at their organisation, but taking a systems thinking approach considering the broader world in which we operate.

Use caution when applying Warrior Leadership

While applying the Warrior Leadership model, it is important to remember that it is a situational leadership approach along an Ownership Continuum. This continuum consists of two distinct styles located at opposite ends.

The leader must possess the capability to read the situation and adjust orientation along the Ownership Continuum accordingly. The situation cannot change on its own, it requires the leader to adapt his leadership approach to match the current circumstances. This requires the ability for the leader to change from a hands-off to a hands-on approach should the demand arise.

Taking courageous action or implementing change always entails the possibility of unintended consequences. Failing to address these consequences could have severe repercussions, potentially derailing the original change objective and eroding the leader's credibility in the process. In extreme situations, unintended consequences could result in chaos and turmoil, causing more harm than good.

The primary leadership style ought to be viewed as Steward Leadership, which inspires a culture of Ownership for all. Even during trying times when the leader assumes Total Ownership, this is done solely to reestablish the setting for Shared Ownership. The leader's ability to inspire Shared Ownership during regular business operations is what cultivates the trust necessary for them to be entrusted with assuming Total Ownership during a crisis. The leader can execute with zero trust and create the illusion of results. However, for engaged and supportive people, trust is essential and serves as 'political muscle' to accomplish tasks with the backing of the people.

Conclusion

The Steward Leader responsibly manages and develops resources, by prioritising long-term sustainability and recognises his role as a caretaker for the benefit of society and the organisation. Whereas the Warrior Leader provides protection through direction, stability and support during uncertainty. Effective Steward-Warrior Leadership builds resilient, empowered and adaptable organisations.

To enable effective leadership in this challenging new world, the *Rise of the Warrior Leader* provides a new approach to leadership. This Ownership-driven Leadership approach builds on previous models, in order to facilitate the application of these principles in daily living.

To execute this approach there are important building blocks to have in place:

Safety (physical and psychological)

Providing physiological safety is a fundamental human need that must be met before anything else. After that, psychological safety becomes crucial, with the leader taking Ownership of the responsibility to hold the space.

Inclusive leadership

There needs to be a culture of inclusion, for people to feel a sense of belonging and cohesion. This involves practicing active listening and making individuals feel valued and respected. This includes creating a safe and supportive environment where individuals feel comfortable sharing their thoughts and ideas and where the leader can respond with empathy and understanding. By prioritising active listening and creating a culture of respect and inclusivity, leaders can build stronger relationships with their team members and foster a more collaborative and productive work environment.

Shared Values and Shared Vision

To build a values-driven culture, people must grasp how their actions can either align with or deviate from their vision, resulting in a raised awareness of the impact of their choices. This understanding empowers individuals to make decisions that align with their values and promote a positive culture.

These building blocks align with Maslow's hierarchy of needs.

Figure 45
Ownership-driven life for the Collective:
Inspiring a life of purpose and meaning

Source: © C. Chiste 2022

* Ownership-driven Leadership aims to raise people to the top of Maslow's hierarchy, promoting self-sufficiency and a sense of stakeholdership. This enables an **Ownership-driven life** from the people's perspective.

The Sanskrit term *'Svadeshi'* gained prominence during the Indian Independence Movement and is often translated roughly as being "of one's own country". However, a more accurate translation is that of self-sufficiency, the feeling of being an empowered stakeholder in one's country.

Note: The values level refers to a values-driven life to support one's purpose, even if the purpose is only to put bread on the table. Purpose can also be considered a higher purpose when it contributes to a greater good, fostering a sense of Ownership and motivating individuals with a deeper sense of meaning and fulfillment in their organisation or country.

Transactional Leadership primarily addresses physiological safety, to an extent also providing a sense of belonging by virtue of people being part of an organisation. However, Transactional Leadership falls short in addressing the need for personal empowerment and purpose. The subsequent levels of the hierarchy relate to psychological needs. The first being the need to have a sense of belonging. This is the essence of **Inclusive Culture-driven Leadership**. An example which has gained international attention in recent years, is the South African concept of **Ubuntu Leadership**. The next level is **Values-driven Leadership**. This draws upon a conscious commitment by the Collective to 'live' their values. This creates a culture that optimises performance, ethical practice, social contribution and environmental consideration. The question to ask oneself is, "Will my actions, no matter how small, take me towards my goals?" At the top of the pyramid is Ownership-driven Leadership, providing individuals with a sense of internal locus of control by understanding their why and empowering them to pursue it. This sense of control is essential for mental toughness and resilience. With a sense of Ownership, individuals feel invested in the outcome of their tasks.

Figure 46
Ownership-driven Leadership for the Leader:
The concept of Ownership takes on a selfless dimension

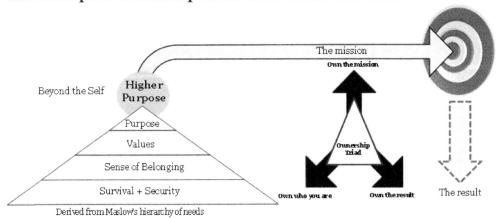

Source: © C. Chiste 2022

This is Ownership from the leader's perspective, with the mission falling within the parameters of the Warrior and Steward Leader. Ownership-driven Leadership entails believing in your people and ensuring safety, in terms of both physical and psychological safety.

Acknowledging the contribution from people for them to feel like stakeholders, whilst developing and empowering them. In taking ownership of the mission, the situation may demand a change in leadership style, requiring the leader to change orientation on the Ownership Continuum. The key difference between the two previous diagrams is that the latter takes on a selfless dimension. For those who are not yet ready to serve and lead, Figure 45 applies. However, for both these diagrams the principle of an Ownership-driven life remains:

Own who you are. Own the mission. Own the result.

The harsh reality is that one day the leader will invariably be faced with a challenge so great that courageous action will be required. Even though the Steward-Warrior Leader is trusted by the Collective, the leader may encounter opposition from the very people he is seeking to protect. A simplified graphic representation of the five key components of Ownership-driven Leadership consists of the Ownership Triad, with the component concerning the mission being within the framework of Warrior-Steward Leadership along the Ownership Continuum.

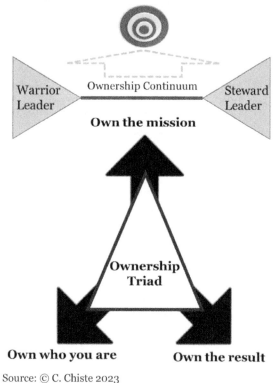

Figure 47
Ownership-driven Leadership: A simplified overview

Source: © C. Chiste 2023

This model uses visual aids to help leaders form mental images, making it easier to apply its concepts. During my military training, I learned 15 principles of leadership and management, but in high-pressure situations, it may be difficult to recall and apply them appropriately. However, with the help of graphics, the model's conceptual framework can be easily recalled and applied when needed.

In a world plagued by uncertainty, leaders must possess additional dimensions to become a 'force for good'. They must take Ownership in an increasingly disruptive global environment, where events such as Covid-19 or cyber-attacks have become the new norm, to ensure that there is no Ownership vacuum. With climate change, economic, energy, political and social-related challenges expected to bring more disruptions in the future, leaders need to enhance their skills to navigate uncertainty effectively. These new challenges require a new approach to leadership: Ownership-driven Leadership underpinned by Selflessness. To be both a Steward and Warrior Leader. **The time is now.**

It's time for the *Rise of the Warrior Leader.*

Bonus Section

The contents of this bonus section are expanded upon in my book *Mental Toughness of a Warrior*. Consider this a preview.

"If you know the enemy and know yourself, you need not fear the result of a hundred battles.

If you know yourself but not the enemy, for every victory gained you will also suffer a defeat.

If you know neither the enemy nor yourself, you will succumb in every battle."

Sun Tzu, The Art of War

Knowing oneself is the first step in leadership. The SPEAR[10] coaching model is a technique that helps leaders become more conscious of their intentions, align their actions with their goals, whilst building mental toughness and resilience. This framework empowers leaders to effectively lead the Collective and improves their leadership abilities.

Figure 48
The SPEAR model as a coaching model for Self-Leadership

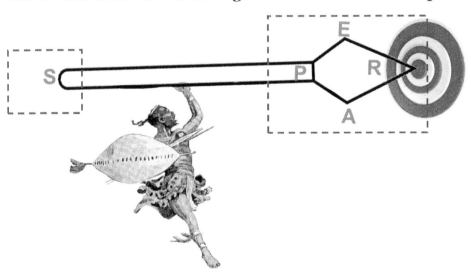

Source: C. Chiste 2020.
Credit: The impi was sketched by Boy Scout Movement founder, Sir Robert Baden-Powell 1913.

---

[10] The SPEAR model introduced in 2020 by Claudio Chiste takes inspiration from the GROW model and the US Navy Seal's "Big Four" of Mental Toughness. GROW is a renowned coaching framework introduced by Sir John Whitmore in the late 1980s, aimed at helping to develop human potential towards a goal. The US Navy Seal's Big "Four" relates to mental rehearsal, micro-goals, emotion and attention management.

Note: The preceding diagram illustrates how a leader engages in self-management while pursuing the desired Result (R) through his chosen Path (P). The process begins with the leader being aware of both his own needs and the needs of the people being led. This heightened awareness of Self (S) allows the leader to ensure that his leadership intentions are aligned with the needs of the people. Maintaining focus along the Path is crucial, and this is achievable through effective self-management involving both Attention Management (A) and Emotion Management (E).

Breakdown of SPEAR acronym:

S - Self

This requires possessing self-awareness and awareness of the Collective, including emotional intelligence, familiarity with the culture(s) and values of the Collective. Strengthening the human connection further enhances resilience and fosters a sense of belonging.

P – Path

To attain the desired Result, it is necessary to follow a specific Path. The leader must possess the skill to navigate the Ownership Continuum, depending on the situation. To enhance leadership effectiveness, extensive research involving 17,000 evaluations of C-suite executives has identified four influential behaviours. Successful CEOs are statistically associated with the following four behaviours: decisiveness, impactful engagement, bold adaptation, and unwavering reliability.

E – Emotion Management

The leader continues doing 'inner work' to take/maintain ownership of who he is, understanding his purpose to enable ownership of the mission and the consequences of his actions. This could be facilitated by physical exercise, leadership coaching and varying self-regulating techniques such as breathwork, self-reflection and meditation.

A – Attention Management

This is the practice of controlling distractions to ensure being present. Your mind is constantly processing information. This information could be related to things which will take you to your goals, or merely distractions for ephemeral pleasure. Pareto's principle, also referred to as the 80/20 Rule, tells us that 80% of the result is often due to 20% of the effort. By eliminating distractions and thoughts which do not serve you, attention can be focused on leveraging the 80/20 Rule.

R - Result

This is the desired Result, consisting primarily of the vision, whilst raising consciousness and ensuring safety.

Figure 49
SPEAR model link to the Ownership and Safety Continuum: Personal and Professional Leadership Framework

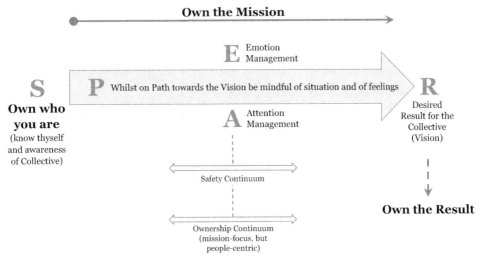

Source: © C. Chiste 2020

This expanded SPEAR model has an enhanced focus on Emotion Management and Attention Management, incorporating the Safety and Ownership Continuum. Emotion Management involves continuous self-reflection and ownership of Self. The leader's belief in the mission also helps the leader to regulate emotions during challenging times.

Avoiding negative influences is crucial as they can cause intense emotional reactions that are difficult to regulate and may interfere with one's goal, resulting in a downward emotional spiral. Avoiding negative influences can improve emotion and attention management by reducing adverse responses that impair clear thinking. However, it's important to approach challenging situations being mindful of the selfless intention behind the desired Result, having effective strategies for Emotion and Attention Management.

Emotion Management

AVOID forcing triggers and negative thoughts into submission.	OWN who you are. This involves owning your Shadow.
AVOID taking on extremely challenging tasks without knowing why you are doing it.	OWN the mission. This involves owning mission critical values, for this to become part of your own personal mission. Sheer willpower is not enough. You need to believe in the mission and understand how adherence to the associated values serve you.
AVOID impulsive decision-making when things don't work.	OWN the result/consequences. This involves having acceptance of the outcome and an awareness of the consequences of your action. How will my decision serve the purpose?

Attention Management

AVOID obsessively focusing on the problem and what is wrong. There is a saying, "where the mind goes, the energy flows."	Maintain the big picture of where you are in the mission, this being the Path towards the Result. **Safety Continuum** assessment. What is the wellbeing of the Collective, be it physically, emotionally or mentally? Do the people feel safe? In addition to the leader focusing on the HOW of leadership and Shadow management, enabled by the Systems Leadership Equation.

The SPEAR model enhances the leader's character, resilience and intellect.

Figure 50

Steward-Warrior Leadership requirements model: The Leadership Wheel interplay with Ownership

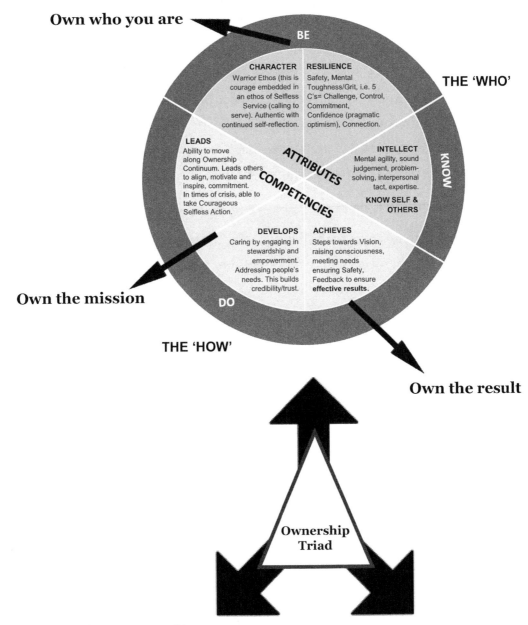

Source: Adapted from US Army, C. Chiste 2021

Revisiting the Leadership Wheel, we see the interplay with the three components of Ownership.

Meaning behind the Centre for Leadership logo

The logo contains four key representational features:

1.   A solid foundation

The square (angled, resembling a diamond) signifies a solid
foundation. The ancient pyramids may be commonly associated
with a triangular shape, but they are actually built on a solid
square base. This serves as a powerful reminder that a strong
foundation is crucial in achieving any goal in life. It is not enough
to simply start; one must also persist and keep working towards
the life they want to live. In freemasonry, the square is a symbol for regulating
life and correcting character weaknesses in search of inner harmony.

2.   Shadow observance

Notice that there are actually two squares. The upper square is how we show up
in the world, the lower square represents our Shadow. It is ever present, yet that
is not the side we show to the world.

3.   A purpose-driven life

The upward-pointing solid triangle gives the impression of directing towards
the upper square in a manner similar to an arrow. As it points to the upper
square, it is a metaphor for showing up with a purpose, not letting your
Shadow dominate.

4.   Alignment of True, Actual and Ideal Self

The three vertical lines beneath the triangle resemble the shaft of the arrow.
These represent the concept of the three Selfs: True, Actual and Ideal Self. Even
though these three are separate, all are aligned towards your purpose. Without
this alignment, you are not living in harmony with who you are.

List of Graphics

Reading List:
Academic Papers

Algera, P. M., Lips-Wiersma, M. (2012). Radical authentic leadership: co-creating the conditions under which all members of the organization can be authentic. Leadership Quarterly 23: 118–131.

Avolio B.J., Gardner W.L. (2005). Authentic leadership development: getting to the root of positive forms of leadership. Leadership Quarterly 16: 315–338.

Barrick, M. R., & Mount, M. K. (1991). The big five personality dimensions and job performance: A meta-analysis. Personnel Psychology, 44, 1–26.

Bass, B. M., Steidlmeier, P. (1999). Ethics, character, and authentic transformational leadership. Leadership Quarterly 10: 181–217.

Bass, B.M., Avolio, B.J. (1990). Developing transformational leadership: 1992 and beyond. Journal of European Industrial Training, 14: 21-27.

Burke R. J (2006) 'Why leaders fail: exploring the darkside', International Journal of Manpower, Vol. 27 Issue 1: 91–100.

Digman, J. M. (1990). Personality structure: Emergence of the five-factor model. Annual Review of Psychology, 41, 417–440.

Doraiswamy, I., R. (2012). Servant or Leader? Who will stand up please? International Journal of Business and Social Science. Vol. 3 No. 9 : 178-182.

Eva, N., Robin, M., Sendjaya, S., van Dierendonck, D., Liden, R., C. (2019). Servant Leadership: A systematic review and call for future research. The Leadership Quarterly. Volume 30, Issue 1, February 2019: Pages 111-132.

Farling, M.L., Stone, A.G., Winston, B.E. (1999). Servant leadership: setting the stage for empirical research. Journal of Leadership Studies, 6, 49-72.

Gandolfini, F., Stone, S. (2016). Clarifying Leadership: High-impact Leaders in a Time of Leadership Crisis. Review of International Comparative Management. Volume 17, Issue3 July 2016: 212-224.

Garcia, Helio Fred. (2006). Effective Leadership Response to Crisis. Strategy & Leadership 34 (1): 4-10.

Gardner W.L., Avolio B.J., Luthans F, May D.R., Walumbwa F. (2005). Can you see the real me? A self-based model of authentic leader and follower development, The Leadership Quarterly: 16(3): 343–72.

Gatling, A., Harrah, W.F. (2014). The Authentic Leadership Qualities of Business Coaches and Its Impact on Coaching Performance. International Journal of Evidence Based Coaching and Mentoring, 12(1): 27-46.

House, R.J. (1971). A path-goal theory of leadership effectiveness. Administrative Science Quarterly. 16: 321–328.

House, R. J., Wright, N. S., & Aditya, R. N. (1997). Cross-cultural research on organizational leadership: A critical analysis and a proposed theory. In P. C. Earley & M. Erez (Eds.), New Perspectives in International Industrial

Organizational Psychology (pp. 535-625). San Francisco: New Lexington.

Howell, J. M., Avolio, B. J. (1993). The ethics of charismatic leadership: Submission or liberation? Academy of Management Executive, 6(2): 43–54.

Ibarra, H., Scoular, A. (2015). The authenticity paradox: why feeling like a fake can be a sign of growth. Harvard Business Review 93: 52–59.

James, E. H., Wooten, L., P. (2005). Leadership as (Un)usual: How to Display Competence in Times of Crisis. Organizational Dynamics 34 (2): 141-52.

Joseph, E. E., Winston, B. E. (2005). A correlation of servant leadership, leader trust & organizational trust. Leadership & Organization Development Journal 26.

Judge, T. A., Bono, J. E., Ilies, R., & Gerhardt, M. (2002). Personality and leadership: A qualitative and quantitative review. Journal of Applied Psychology, 87, 765–780.

Jung, D. I. (2001). Transformational and transactional leadership and their effects on creativity in groups. Creativity Research Journal 13: 185–195.

Lewin, K., and Lippit, R. (1938). An experimental approach to the study of autocracy and democracy: a preliminary note. Sociometry 1: 292–300.

Lynch, J. A., Friedman, H. H. (2013). Servant leader, spiritual leader: The case for convergence. Journal of Leadership, Accountability and Ethics, 10(2): 87-95.

McCuddy, M. K., Cavin, M. C. (2008). Fundamental moral orientations, servant leadership, and leadership effectiveness: An empirical test. Review of Business Research, 8(4): 107-117.

Nhung-Binh Ly (2020): Cultural Influences on Leadership: Western-Dominated Leadership and Non-Western Conceptualizations of Leadership, Sociology and Anthropology 8(1): 1-12.

Peus, C., Wesche, J.S., Streicher, B., Braun, S. Frey, D. (2012). Authentic Leadership: An Empirical Test of Its Antecedents, Consequences, and Mediating Mechanisms. Journal of Business Ethics, 107: 331-348.

Prewitt, J. E., Weil, R. (2014). Organizational Opportunities Endemic in Crisis Leadership. Journal of Management Policy and Practice, 15(2): 72-87.

Robertson, I., Cooper, C. L., Sarkar, M., & Curran, T. (2015). Resilience training in the workplace from 2003-2014: A systematic review. Journal of Occupational and Organizational Psychology, 88, 533-562.

Rowe, A. (2016). Managing a Crisis: Leadership and Organizational Elements Essential for Success. Submitted to the System Design and Management Program in partial fulfilment of the requirements for the degree of Master of Science in Engineering and Management Massachusetts Institute of Technology.

Samad, S. (2012). The influence of Innovation & Transformational Leadership on Organizational Performance. Procedia Social and Behavioural Sciences 57: 486- 493.

Schwab, D. P. (1980). Construct validity in organizational behavior. In L. L. Cummings & B.M. Staw (Eds.), Greenwich: JAI Press, Research in organizational behavior, Vol. 2: 3–43.

Sendjaya, S. (2003). Development and validation of servant leadership behavioral scale. Servant Leadership Roundtable. Virginia Beach, VA: Regent University.

Sendjaya, S., Cooper, B. (2011). Servant leadership behavior scale: A hierarchical model and test of construct validity. European Journal of Work and Organizational Psychology, 20(3): 416–436.

Sendjaya, S., Pekerti, A. (2010). Servant leadership as antecedent of trust in organizations. Leadership & Organization Development Journal, 31(7): 643–663.

Sendjaya, S., Sarros, J. C., Santora, J. C. (2008). Defining and measuring servant leadership behavior in organizations. Journal of Management Studies, 45(2): 402–424.

Strang, K.D. (2005). Examining effective and ineffective transformational project leadership. Team Performance Management: An International Journal, 11 (3/4): 68 – 103.

Triandis, H. C. (1989). The self and social behavior in differing cultural contexts. Psychological Review, 96(3): 506–520.

Vito, G.F., Higgins, G.E., Denney, A.S. (2014). 'Transactional and transformational leadership,' Policing: An International Journal of Police Strategies & Management, 37 (4): 809 – 822.

Walumbwa, F., Avolio, B., Gardner, W., Wernsing, T., & Peterson, S. (2008). Authentic Leadership: Development and Validation of a Theory-Based Measure. Journal of Management, 34(1): 89-126.

Wilson, K. R. (2010). Steward leadership: characteristics of the steward leader in Christian non-profit organizations. A Dissertation Presented for the Degree of PhD. The University of Aberdeen.

Wooten, L.P., James, E.H., Parsons, K. (2013). Handbook of Research on Crisis Leadership in Organizations. Edward Elgar Publishing, Cheltenham.

Wort, A. R. (2012). Development and evaluation of a Professional Leadership Development Model. A Dissertation Presented for the Degree of PhD. The University of Johannesburg.

Yoshida, D., T., Sendjaya, S., Hirst, G., Cooper, B. (2014). Does servant leadership foster creativity and innovation? A multi-level mediation study of identification and prototypicality. Journal of Business Research 67: 1395- 1404.

Books

April, K., Kukard, J., Peters, K. (2014). Steward Leadership: A Maturational Perspective. South Africa: UCT Press.

Abdullah S., M. (1995). The Power of One: Authentic Leadership in Turbulent Times. Philadelphia: New Society Publishers.

Barkow, J., Cosmides, L. Tooby, J. (1992). The adapted mind: Evolutionary psychology and the generation of culture. Oxford: Oxford University Press.

Barret, R. (2010). The new leadership paradigm. Richard Barret.

Bass, B. M. (1990). Bass and Stogdill's handbook of leadership. New York: Free Press.

Bass, B. M., Riggio, R. E. (2006). Transformational leadership (2nd ed). Mahwah, NJ: Lawrence Erlbaum.

Bass, B.M. (1985). Leadership and performance beyond expectations. New York: Free Press.

Botelho, E. L., Powell, K. R., Tahl, R. (2018). The CEO Next Door. New York: Penguin Random House.

Burns, J. M. (1978). Leadership. New York: Harper & Row.

Clark, Timothy, R. (2020). The 4 Stages of Psychological Safety: Defining the Path to Inclusion and Innovation. USA. Penguin.

Cleary, T. (1999). Ways of Warriors, Codes of Kings: Lessons in Leadership from the Chinese Classics. USA. Shambhala Publication.

Collins, J. (2001). Good to Great. New York: HarperCollins.

Covey, S. (2004). The 8th Habit. UK. Simon & Schuster UK Ltd.

Craig, N., George, B. & Snook, S. (2015). The Discover Your True North Fieldbook: A Personal Guide to Finding Your Authentic Leadership. New Jersey, Wiley.

Cross, R., Miles, R. (2011). Warrior Women: 3,000 Years of Courage and Heroism. London (UK): Quercus Publishing Plc.

Divine, M. (2013). The way of the SEAL. China: Readers Digest.

Fiedler, F. E. (1967). A theory of leadership effectiveness. New York: McGraw-Hill.

Fink, S. (1986). Crisis management: Planning for the inevitable. New York: Amacom.

George, B., Sims, P. (2007). True north: Discover your authentic leadership. San Francisco, CA: Jossey-Bass.

George, W. (2003). Authentic leadership: rediscovering the secrets to creating lasting value. San Francisco (CA): Jossey-Bass.

Goleman, D., Boyatzis, R., McKee, A. (2002). Primal leadership: Realizing the power of emotional intelligence. Boston: Harvard Business School Press.

Graumann, C.F., & Moscovici, S. (1986). Changing conceptions of leadership, New York: Springer-Veriag.

Greenleaf, R. K. (1970). The servant as leader. Robert K. Greenleaf Publishing Center.

Greenleaf, R. K. (1977). Servant leadership. New York, Paulist Press.

Gronski, John. L (2021). Iron-Sharpened Leadership. USA, Fidelis Publishing.

Goleman, D. (1995). Emotional intelligence: Why it can matter more than IQ? New York: Bantam Books.

Goleman, D., Boyatzis, R., McKee, A. (2002). Primal leadership: Realizing the power of emotional intelligence. Boston: Harvard Business School Press.

Hollander E (1978). Leadership Dynamics. New York: Free Press.

Jacobi, J. (1965). The way of individuation. New York: Harcourt, Brace & World Inc.

Jung, C.G (1982). Aspects of the Feminine. NY. Princeton University Press.

Klann, G. (2003). Crisis Leadership: Using Military Lessons, Organizational Experiences. USA. CCL Press.

Kouzes, J. Posner, B. (2007). The Leadership Challenge (4th ed). San Francisco: Jossey-Bass.

Laloux, F. (2014). Reinventing Organisations. USA. Knowledge Resources Publishing Pty Ltd.

Marquet, David, l. (2015). *Turn Your Ship Around!* USA: First published by Portfolio / Penguin, a member of Penguin group (USA) LLC.

Mitroff II. (2004). Crisis leadership: Planning for the unthinkable. Hoboken, NJ: Wiley.

Mol, A. (2012). Creating Winners in the workplace. South Africa. Christian Art Publishers

Patterson, K. (2004). Servant leadership: A theoretical Model. Servant Leadership Research Roundtable, Virginia Beach, VA.

Perkins, D.N.T, Holtman, M. P., Kessler, P., MCCarthy, C. (2012 2nd Ed). Leading at the Edge: Leadership Lessons from the Extraordinary Saga of Shackleton's Antarctic Expedition. USA. AMACOM.

Shankman M., & Allen, S. J. (2008). Emotionally intelligent leadership: A guide for college students. San Francisco, CA: Jossey-Bass.

Terry, R, W. (1993). Authentic Leadership: Courage in Action. USA. Jossey- Bass Inc. Publishers.

Tzu, Sun: Alexander, B. (2011). *Sun Tzu at Gettysburg*. New York. W.W. Norton & Company.

Villani S. (1999). Are you sure you're principal? On being an authentic leader. Thousand Oaks (CA): Corwin Press.

Willink, J., & Babin, L. (2015). Extreme Ownership. USA. St. Partin's Press.

Articles

Bahnsen, J. C., Cone, R. W. (1990). Defining the American Warrior Leader. US Army College.

Firestone, S. (2020). What is Crisis Leadership? Biblical Principles of Crisis Leadership. 2020: 7–21. Published online 29 May 2020.

Knight, Andrew. J. (2014). Retaining the Warrior Spirit. Military Review. September-October 2014: 88-100.

Poon, R. A. (2006). Model for Servant Leadership and Mentorship. School of Leadership Studies, Regent University. Servant Leadership Research Roundtable. August 2006.

Pullen, B., Crane, E. (2011). Creating a Coaching Culture in a Global Organization. The International Journal of Coaching in Organizations. Issue 30,8 (2): 5-19.

Riccio, G, Sullivan, R, Klein, G, Salter, M & Kinnison, H. (2004). Warrior Ethos: Analysis of the Concept and Initial Development of Applications. The Wexford Group International. Research Report 1827. September 2004.

Scott, B. B. (1993). A Sapiential Performance of an Apocalyptic Discourse. In Search of Wisdom: Essays in Memory of John G. Gammie (L. G. Perdue, B. B. Scott, W. J. Wiseman, Ed.) (1st ed). Louisville, KY: Westminster John Knox Press: 245-263.

Winston, B. (2003). Extending Patterson's Servant Leadership Model: Coming Full Circle. Regent University School of Leadership Studies Servant Leadership Research Roundtable. 16 October 2003.

Wong, L., Kolditz, T.A., Millen, R. A., Potter, T. M (2003). Why they fight: Combat motivation in the Iraq War. Carlisle, PA: Strategic Studies Institute, US Army War College. July 2003.

Acknowledgements

Let me first acknowledge my foundational training which was forged in the military. In the South African Navy, I served when the system was not burdened by present day political imperatives, with 'brutal lessons' raising my awareness of the harsh reality that nothing is guaranteed. A case in point being the four-day Navy divers selection which was relentless, to say the least. From the 90 men that took part in the grueling selection, I was fortunate to be one of the only three successful candidates.

Thanks to my proofreader, Bruno Bruniquel, who provided sound input, consistently reminding me that 'less is more' when conveying a message. His eagle eyes served me to challenge and reinforce my own thinking. Thanks to Dawn Klatzko for inspiring me to 'own' my message.

Special mention to my mentor whilst in the Navy, Rear Admiral (jg) (retd) S. F. Petersen, an officer who served in the Marines and the first 'Coloured' Officer Commanding of a South African warship. He taught me the valuable lesson that to expect the best, you would first need to prepare for the worst. It was an honour to serve and be the Parade Commander for the decommissioning of the torpedo recovery vessel and diving tender, SAS FLEUR (P3148). She was the first metal ship built in South Africa after WW2 and commonly known as the 'workhorse of the Navy'. For those that served on her she was affectionately called the Mighty Fluff. As a consequence of her instability in rough seas, at times she was sometimes jocularly called the 'vomit comet'. At the time of her historic decommissioning, Commander S. de Boer was the Officer Commanding.

My university professor, Professor Costas Grammenos CBE, the Chairman of the 'Costas Grammenos Centre for Shipping, Trade and Finance', Bayes Business School (formerly Cass Business School), City, University of London deserves special mention. The Prof, as he is affectionately known, played a key role in my transition from the Navy to the corporate world of specialist and investment banking.

Gratitude to Mark Brownrigg OBE for his support of the next generation of shipping professionals whilst the UK Chamber of Shipping Director General, and I was the newly elected Chairman of the Shipping Professional Network in London (SPNL). University of Monaco's Professor Guy Morel, who was then president of the Monaco-based MC Shipping. True to the original Latin meaning of the word 'inspire', Yannick Le Gouriérès, Gustav Ellingsen and Dr Simon Norton, your energies helped bring life to the projects we collaborated on. Gratitude to all those not mentioned who walked with me on my journey, you know who you are. Not to mention Dr Gary van Vuuren for his role in this transition.

Great appreciation to Intesa Sanpaolo's Federico Barlozzetti and Alessandro Vitale who helped me develop as an international banker, not to mention Richard Zatta and Michele Dapri who provided solid leadership. Thanks to Dr Sendjaya for sharing research material, Mark Wiley, Dr Sunny Stout-Rostron, Dumisani Ntuli, Marc Fletcher, Monique Strauss and Andrew Trainor for honest feedback. Sumi "Sassy" Engelbrecht for all your magical care. Lucille Greeff - the timeous gifting of the book *Steward Leadership* was well received. Gratitude to Investec, especially the organisation development staff (known as the OD team) who were on hand to ensure a culture underpinned by shared values. Steve Torr, who is a shining example of values in action with an in depth understanding of leadership through service. Not to mention Gary Laughton and Ciaran Whelan, where my awareness was raised to Decentralised Command in a corporate context, being introduced to Ricardo Semler's leadership philosophy. This philosophy is about providing people the freedom to operate. However, this 'freedom' comes with the understanding that, with any risk undertaken, there is also the associated responsibility and accountability.

Deep gratitude to my father, Diego, who embedded a mindset of resilience from a young age and the power of: 'do what you must do', not taking the easy path. My mother, Sophia (Saffia), provided me with a solid foundation and intuition ability. My sister, Rosalba, and to my grandmother Selma (Jaja) for their role in shaping me during my upbringing. Finally, to my wife Jessica, in supporting me on my entrepreneurial adventure journey, which is not for the faint hearted. Above all, utmost gratitude to the one and only Almighty.

Author biography

Claudio is a Director of the Centre for Leadership. He serves as the President of the Cape Chapter of the Professional Speakers Association of Southern Africa (PSASA) and the Chairman of Coaches & Mentors of South Africa (Comensa) for the Western Cape, previously serving on the Social & Ethics Committee. He is a certified Master NLP Practitioner and Master Life Coach, carrying the industry respected designation Comensa Credentialed Coach. He has completed Assessor and Moderator accreditation training.

Claudio's intrinsic values have influenced his belief in making a difference for the common good, by helping others to adopt a mindset of resilience, and engendering a culture which embraces leadership, regardless of seniority. Claudio is a firm believer that nothing is instant, only instant coffee, results take time. The important thing is to progress, setting habitual micro-goals on a daily basis.

His varied background allows him to have a multi-angled approach, with a background as a leader whilst a combat officer in the South African Navy (9 years), and as a specialist banker in London (10 years) with the Italian banking giant, Intesa Sanpaolo and the Anglo-South African Investec Bank. During this period, he was in charge of an international award-wining business association focused on promoting both business and the next generation, called Shipping Professional Network London (www.spnl.co.uk) serving as chairman for 8 years. He has received numerous industry awards, including Business Leader of the Year award (SA Chamber of Commerce) and the New Leader of the Year (Crans Montana, Switzerland).

Claudio has a Master of Science from Bayes Business School (formerly Cass Business School), the business school of the City, University of London, B. Comm (Hons) from University of Cape Town and a Bachelor in Military Science majoring in 'pure' Mathematics and Nautical Science from the South African Military Academy, Stellenbosch University.

As a giveback to his community, he has been a business leader on the Partners for Possibility programme, currently a trauma volunteer with a crisis intervention organisation (CIC) and serves on the EXCO of his local Community Police Forum (CPF) where he oversees leadership and mental resilience workshops with schools to help uplift and bring the community together.